DISCARDED

Whad'ya Knowledge?

Whad'ya Know?

Whad'ya Knowledge?

Michael Feldman

WILLIAM MORROW AND COMPANY, INC. | NEW YORK

It is a policy of William Morrow and Company, Inc., and its imprints and affiliates, recognizing the importance of preserving what has been written, to print the books we publish on acid-free paper, and we exert our best efforts to that end.

Library of Congress Cataloging-in-Publication Data

Feldman, Michael, 1949–
    Whad'ya knowledge? / Michael Feldman.
        p.   cm.
    ISBN 0-688-10796-6
    1. American wit and humor.   I. Title.   II. Title: Whad' ya
knowledge?
    PN6162.F392   1993   818'.5402—dc20   92-32421
                                                                CIP

Printed in the United States of America

First Edition

1 2 3 4 5 6 7 8 9 10

BOOK DESIGN BY BARBARA M. BACHMAN

TITLE PAGE PHOTOGRAPH BY ANTHONY LOEW

For my better halves,

Consuela and Consuelita

Contents

THINGS YOU SHOULD HAVE LEARNED IN SCHOOL

(HAD YOU BEEN PAYING ATTENTION) ● 99

SCIENCE ● *132*

ODDS AND ENDS ● *175*

AFTERWORD

LEARNING THEORY AND PRACTICE ● *216*

Introduction

● **THE HANDWRITING IS ON THE WALL** —and the spelling suks! Two out of three of our students—let's see, that's 75 percent!—have deficient math skills, and most cannot point to themselves on a map even if they're standing on it. Many high-school seniors have no idea that North Dakota and South Dakota are adjacent, and would be shocked to hear about the Carolinas. True, many are on the Zonk level on Zarastran, making them eligible to spend the rest of their semiwaking hours in one level or another of Super Nintendo hell, but do they know that a hard-boiled egg can be sucked into a milk bottle? Do they even care?

Meanwhile, a South Korean kid can figure three years of payments on a Hyundai by the time he's eight, and count on making them by nine. Japanese children annually put in a thousand more hours in school than their American counterparts, even counting detentions. Kids in the former Soviet Union have better geography skills without even having a country. In this country, nobody reads anymore, unless it's his own book, and you see what only a few years ago would have been unthinkable: Bible thumpers whacking videos. People won't even pick up a newspaper, unless it's to see if the cat is under it.

I'm not saying *Whad'ya Knowledge?* is the key to revitalizing the American psyche, making us competitive once again, or restoring the virtues of learning for its own sake and for the sake of creating a more balanced and thoughtful society. But if it inspires even one graffiti artist to spray something thought-provoking with good spelling, maybe we won't have to ban aerosol paint sales to minors. Maybe then we'll require it.

If nothing else, that should wipe out graffiti.

Author's Note

Why This Is
Not Trivia

● **TRIVIA IS NO SMALL THING.** It is, in fact, triv-
ializing the nation: When Americans are not looking
for Waldo they're looking for baby pigeons ("Why do you
never see baby pigeons?") or wondering why they put locks
on the doors of twenty-four-hour convenience stores. While
driving, they're not thinking about road conditions or their
fuzzbusters; their minds are turning over whether or not,
should their Aries approach 176,000 miles per second and
they turn their lights on, they'll be able to see the road.
(Answer: Yes, just remember to use your low beams.) Instead
of enjoying the aesthetics of a winter scene (granted, only the
first snow is aesthetic), they can't help wondering where the
white goes when the snow melts (anyone around here can

tell you: It goes on your shoes, like a milk mustache). Americans, in short, want to know. They just don't want to know anything important. Consider some of the tantalizing questions the audience has come up with on my radio show:

"Does water back up clockwise in the Southern Hemisphere?"

"If you drop a lion from the roof, will it land on its feet?"

"Where are all the Gardol shields from the Colgate commercials?"

"Does a talking vending machine have First Amendment rights?"

"Would a dung beetle eat something else, given a chance?"

"With a moosehead on one side of a Canadian quarter and the queen on the other, which side is 'heads?' "

"Do Jewish people eat corn right to left?"

"Would a sign *requiring* skateboarding be more effective?"

"If a priest, a rabbi, and a nun are in a boat, is there a Congregationalist jumping up and down and waving his arms on the dock?"

"Could God make a word so big William Buckley couldn't flaunt it?"

"Do women live a year longer for every one they hold back?"

"If matter and antimatter meet; will it matter?"

"Do female birds purchase the males' colorful plumage for them?"

None of these questions will be answered here, because what follows is not trivia. It is bigger than that: It's my life. If not kernels of wisdom, these are knowledge nuggets, any one of which can lead to or have led from grants supported by your tax dollar. The answers have all been thoroughly researched, although the questions have not.

Having debunked the trivia rap, I will, however, make the exception to the rule and answer the one question I am most often asked: boxers. They let you breathe.

• Deep Background:

Ordinarily, you would have to be president to receive the kind of thoroughly superficial briefings you will find interspersed in these pages as "Deep Background." Or, if you'd rather be right, somebody—perhaps Kissinger himself—would have to meet you in an underground parking ramp and fill you in, all the while being enigmatic as the sphinx ("Vat valks on vun leg in de morning . . . ?"), and denying it for years afterward, even to Ted Koppel.

Under the "for your eyes only" classification of "Deep Background," you'll find all the details you'll need on the history of bathing to make policy decisions, and the real scoop on why the dinosaurs disappeared so if challenged on the subject, you can give it the right spin. Face it, if you can't be knowledgeable in all things (after all, there is only one Bill Safire, and even he became Spiro Agnew during full moons), it could be of great advantage to you, socially and in a business sense, to appear to know a lot about an obscure subject or two—say the War of Griffin's Pig, or the role of dogs in the Revolutionary War—and leave the impression that there's a lot more where that came from.

And isn't that what being a pundit is all about?

Whad'ya Knowledge?

People

● **PEOPLE ARE ALL RIGHT.** That's easy to forget, being privy to the not-always-endearing idiosyncrasies of one member of the species. Of course, I've got my problems, too.

People are paradoxical, it's true: on the one hand, familiar—constantly addressing you in the second person—and on the other, exotic, or else how could Milwaukee have been featured in *National Geographic* with nobody so much as stripped to the waist? Even the guy edging his lawn was wearing an undershirt, while the South Side ladies sweeping the street with their kitchen brooms (were there bundles of twigs on their backs or am I making that up?) were swaddled right up to their babushkas. It's easy to take your own culture for granted, but the fact is, Margaret Mead could have come of age in Milwaukee, and gotten a deal on Mitchell Street on some togs a bit more appropriate to her age. We are all worthy of study by cultural anthropologists.

Bob F., my friend and college roommate, who was always pretty shy and never went out much, one day (after staying home) decided to become a psychologist. He said he wanted to find out what people were thinking. Now, as a successful shrink in Palo Alto (Spanish for "Go on"), he's still pretty shy and doesn't go out much, probably the result of twenty years of hearing what people were thinking. I'm afraid it may have been a setback.

I hope not, because people, Bob included, really are all right.

---

1. Working parents of teenagers are prime consumers of which of the following?

    a. *over-the-counter sedatives*
    b. *self-stick notes*
    c. *wick-style room deodorizers*

    c. *Quality time, in many households, means* typed *notes. (Mediamark Research)*

2. According to the Gallup poll, what percentage of Americans have a "very high" opinion of lawyers' ethics?

    a. *3 percent*
    b. *2 percent*
    c. *1 percent*

a. *Curiously, about the same percentage as Americans who are lawyers.*

3. When are people over sixty-four likeliest to get the munchies?

    a. *after blowing a little weed*
    b. *in the afternoons*
    c. *right before bed*

c. *According to a* New York Times *poll, snacking strikes in the afternoons for younger people, and gets later in the day as the snackers do.*

4. Out of twenty Americans, how many, when pressed, will mumble something about being shy?

Eight. Barbara Walters, surprisingly, is one. She will not discuss which tree she would be if she were one.

5. What percentage of Americans never throw away junk mail unopened?

    a. *11 percent*
    b. *20 percent*
    c. *30 percent*

b. *Well, it does say "Pay to the order of . . ." (Gallup)*

6. According to Nair, what percentage of American women remove hair from their lower legs regularly?

a. *75 percent*
b. *86 percent*
c. *92 percent*

b. *Nair does not supply figures on American men, but, believe you me, there's more than one.*

7. Women control the checkbook in what number of households?

a. *one out of four*
b. *two out of four*
c. *three out of four*

c. *In the other one, nobody controls the checkbook.* (American Demographics *magazine*)

8. Who is more likely to have tried tofu, a midwesterner or a southerner?

Always up for a new experience is one midwesterner in ten; you'd have to round up twelve southerners before you found a similar example of derring-do. If they deep-fried the stuff and put it next to the pork rinds, you'd see those numbers increase considerably. (Sunset *magazine*)

9. According to the Arthur Murray people, do more people want to fox-trot or mambo?

Overwhelmingly fox-trot (nearly two to one). Swing is still number one, even if it is swing low.

10. According to wives, husbands in which part of the country are the sloppiest?

    a. *South Atlantic (38 percent called "slobs")*
    b. *Northeast (18 percent)*
    c. *West (15 percent)*

    a. *According to the stain-guard people, Monsanto.*

11. What percentage of Americans would use genetic engineering to improve their children?

    a. *2 percent*
    b. *9 percent*
    c. *51 percent*

    b. *Most would be content to simply retouch their graduation pictures. (Harris Poll)*

12. Which age bracket is likeliest to bend over to pick up a penny?

    a. *35 to 49 (72 percent)*
    b. *50 to 64 (84 percent)*
    c. *over 65 (80 percent)*

    b. *My daughter, however, is most likely to pick one up and store it immediately in her mouth.*

13. According to the Harris poll, what percentage of yuppies find their preoccupation with self to be "singularly unattractive"?

    a. *3 percent*
    b. *25 percent*
    c. *90 percent*

    c. *Their preoccupation with introspection notwithstanding.*

14. Out of ten Americans, how many like to be the center of attention?

    a. *one half of one*
    b. *one and one half*
    c. *two*

    b. *Here in the Midwest, people don't even like to have it pointed out that they are not the center of attention.*

15. Who changes their sheets more often, Germans or Spaniards?

    Spaniards, 93 percent of whom change their sheets whether they need to or not. Only 17 percent of Germans do (although this was before reunification, bound to have an impact on linen use).

16. What percentage of Americans never wash their cars?

    a. *15 percent*
    b. *5 percent*
    c. *1 percent*

    b. *There are no figures on how many Americans never renew their vinyl tops, but it must be alarming.*

17. How many cats, out of ten, sometimes do their duty outside the friendly confines of their litter boxes?

    a. *five*
    b. *eight*
    c. *ten*

    a. *I've had cats, and I can't believe its not "c." Maybe I've just had the wrong cats.*

18. What percentage of seventeen-year-old Americans think the Spanish knight who attacked windmills was Zorro?

    a. *15 percent*
    b. *25 percent*
    c. *40 percent*

    a. *Twenty-five percent thought it was Bobby Knight.*

• Deep Background:

Are There Two Types of People in the World?

There are two types of people in the world, those who believe there are two types of people in the world and those who don't. But even among those who believe there are, there is little agreement as to which two. Hippocrates spoke of the *phthisic,* tall, thin, and tubercular, and the *apoplectic,* short, fat, and stroke-prone. Pyramus spoke of those he liked and those he didn't. The poet Coleridge believed that babies were born either Aristotelians or Platonists, depending on whether they were "insies" or "outsies," while Nietzsche saw men as either Apollonian—moderate and orderly conservatives prone to opium use—or Nietzschean, romantic rebels who take a nip now and then.

Sir Francis Galton divided humans into the verbalizers and the visualizers, while the Canadian physican Sir William Osler visualized them as either "larks" or "owls" and probably lived to regret verbalizing it. Jung separated the collectively conscious into introverted Hamlets and extroverted Napoleons, leaving little room for those who want to conquer the world one minute and think about it the next.

One of the more insightful attempts to classify humankind was actually a three-parter dreamed up by the Roman Celsus with his *in vino veritas* types: the "aggressive," who fights when drunk; the "sociable," who dances and sings when drunk; and the "sentimental," who cries. Celsus believed that when sober, men were pretty much an undifferentiated mass.

---

19. What percentage of Americans who buy leotards never work out in them?

  a. *75 percent*
  b. *45 percent*
  c. *25 percent*

  b. *Just getting into them is aerobic for a lot of people.*

20. Would the average person rather have a little work done at the dentist or speak in front of a group?

He/she would rather go to the dentist. Getting people to speak in front of a group of dentists is almost impossible.

21. What is the one modern convenience people say they cannot live without?

    a. *aluminum foil*
    b. *panty hose*
    c. *Scotch tape*

    c. *Scotch tape; you can't live with it, you can't live without it.*

22. According to the American Bar Association, what's the biggest complaint lawyers have about being lawyers?

    a. *Divorcees are not attractive enough*
    b. *They're not making enough money*
    c. *They're expected to laugh at lawyer jokes*

    b. *The average salary in 1990 was only $104,625, hardly the gross national product of Bolivia many had been led to expect.*

23. According to the Waldenbooks Romance Club, do romance-novel readers consider a subway or a blind date a more romantic way to meet a handsome stranger?

The subway—38 percent—is surprisingly romantic to people who never have to descend into one. Only 1 percent

*cited a blind date, and no one, surprisingly, mentioned the
Romance section at Waldenbooks.*

24. According to *Working Mother,* 90 percent of American
parents give allowances. How many dare to expect something
in return?

> a. *10 percent*
> b. *30 percent*
> c. *70 percent*
>
> c. *The rest make allowances.*

25. Does Gallup say that more of us prefer bacon bits or
shredded cheese on our salads?

> *Bacon bits, 48 to 46 percent, so it's really a tossup salad.
> And 72 percent not only expect a tomato, they expect a
> tomato that tastes like one.*

26. What percentage of leftovers in doggie bags actually
make it to a doggie?

> a. *13 percent*
> b. *27 percent*
> c. *39 percent*
>
> a. *But I bet people bags don't make it to people, either.*

27. Who spends less time in the bathroom than their mates?

> a. *men*
> b. *women*
> c. *both*

c. *Two out of three men and women swear they're not in there as much. Can we be talking quality time?*

28. What percentage of Americans get one third of their water intake from beer?

    a. *1 percent*
    b. *3 percent*
    c. *5 percent*

    a. *Slightly higher in Wisconsin.*

29. According to the Saran Wrap people, how many of us have leftovers that are more than four weeks old?

    a. *2 percent*
    b. *5 percent*
    c. *9 percent*

    b. *Two percent don't know how old their leftovers are; 9 percent eat everything and have no leftovers.*

30. Does it just seem that way, or do people really talk longer on pay phones when someone is waiting?

    Yes, according to a study at Georgia State, suggesting that if you are waiting to use a public phone, you'd best crouch behind a dumpster.

31.   Among males, does singing in the shower increase or decrease with age?

One of the few abilities that increases with age, from 16 percent among 21- to 34-year-olds to 50 percent among those 55 and older. Females between 35 and 44 only sing "Respect."

32.   Do more people slurp or twirl their spaghetti?

Twirl, 53 percent to 47 percent, although casual observation suggests a lot of overlapping. There is no difference in rate of slurping among those who refer to it as pasta.

33.   How many Americans say work interferes with their leisure?

Half. The rest refuse to let work get in their way. (Roper)

34.   Eighty-two percent of teens around the world can identify the Coca-Cola logo. What percentage can spot the international warning sign for radioactivity?

   a. *7 percent*
   b. *18 percent*
   c. *38 percent*

   c. *In the interests of safety, the Coca-Cola logo should be made the international symbol for radioactivity. (*American Demographics*)*

35.   What percentage of people who shop through catalogs don't know why?

   a. *2 percent*
   b. *10 percent*
   c. *20 percent*

c. *At least the little voice is not telling them to "kill."*

36. Which of the following do Americans rate as the best value?

    a. *college tuition*
    b. *compact discs*
    c. *chicken*

    c. *College tuition is called a good value by 12.4 percent, CDs 9.3 percent—but chicken rates 40.4 percent. My mother wants to remind you to look for a nice yellow one.*

37. According to the Korbel champagne people, what percentage of married people say they have gone to bed angry "many times"?

    a. *33⅓ percent*
    b. *around half*
    c. *85 percent*

    c. *And 15 percent, I guess, have a little Korbel.*

38. How many teenagers listen to music with blatantly destructive themes?

    a. *17 percent*
    b. *24 percent*
    c. *33 percent*

    a. *This, according to the University of Florida, rises to 41 percent among juvenile delinquents—still a minority—*

suggesting a frightening possibility: juvenile delinquents on easy-listening music.

• Deep Background:

What's in a Name?

While given names may reflect a predilection for romance novels or mellifluous-sounding household products, surnames often stem from accolades or abuse heaped upon our ancestors generations ago. Many English names, for example, are flotsam and jetsam from the Norman invasion, French places and personages upon which the English take what revenge they can by misspelling and mispronouncing them. The town of Montfort-Sur-Risle in Normandy, for example, begat the Montforts, Montfords, Mountfords, Mundfords, and Mumfords, all of whom mistakenly believe they're as English as kippers.

Occupations provided a large body of surnames: Taylors, Glovers, Saddlers, Cooks, Butlers, Barbers, Bakers, and so on, but here, as well, a rose is not always a rose. The name Marshall, for example, which one might assume to have some status, actually refers to the servant who marshaled guests into the drawing room, while Steward comes from sty-ward, or keeper of the pigs. Nicknames were popular in the Middle Ages, and, fortunately for succeeding generations, not all of them stuck: Cruikshank, Handless, Onehand, Neck, Blind, Daft, Mutter, and Stutter being a few of the kinder notations of physical shortcomings. Even the ones that did stick— names like King, Pope, Abbot, and Duke—may, often as not, have been ironic assessments, so upholding the family name may be a good deal easier than assumed.

For the rest of us, whatever we had been called back in the old country may have fallen on the wooden ear of an Ellis Island official, but, after all, an Aunt Rose by any other name would smell as sweet.

---

39. Out of twenty dog and cat owners, how many have a picture of Smokey or Princess in their wallets?

    a. *four*
    b. *six*
    c. *eight*

    c. *Scary. I almost prefer those with pictures of the household products Pride and Joy.*

40. How many personal products does it take to get the average woman out of the average house on any given morning?

    a. *seven*
    b. *fourteen*
    c. *twenty-one*

    c. *Take away one personal product, the entire hygiene pyramid collapses, and they can't set foot out the door. Men, on the other hand, generally just shave and tweeze the hair off their ears.*

41. Does *Parade* magazine say that religion or driving is more important to Americans over sixty?

Driving, 58 percent to 55 percent, although both would be important to the lady who only drives to church. (Numbers add up to more than 100 percent because Parade's *readership is very large.)*

42. Does a woman's chance of having her message on the family answering machine increase or decrease with age?

Something to live for: increase, *although, according to* The First Really Important Survey of American Habits, *it never gets much better than two to one against. Answering-machine messages provide a technological outlet for the traditional male role of peeing on all the tree stumps around the homestead. This keeps Mary Kay ladies at bay.*

43. What percentage of Arby's customers prefer dealing with computer touch screens to humans?

    a. *39 percent*
    b. *52 percent*
    c. *77 percent*

    c. *After all, when you push a human's face, nothing much happens.*

44. How many people living in the San Francisco Bay area believe "people are able to transform their level of consciousness to more fully realize their human potential by using certain kinds of meditative practices and psychological therapies?"

    a. *99.9 percent*
    b. *74 percent*
    c. *62 percent*

    c. *And a third of them do it, according to a* San Francisco Chronicle-Examiner *poll.*

45. Is a man or a woman more likely to tell you there's toilet paper stuck to your shoe?

    A woman. A man, however, is more likely to tell you there's toilet paper stuck to your shoe when there isn't.

46. How many bananas do you eat a year?

    Fifty. Say woo-woo *and scratch under your arms.*

47. While men and women are equally adept at helping groups solve disputes, women tend to see themselves as "bridges," while men see themselves as what?

    a. *elevated railways*
    b. *lightning rods*
    c. *vises*

    c. *A University of Michigan study reported in* The Wall Street Journal *found that men like to force the two sides together and solder them.*

48. How many Americans, out of ten, hate to entertain?

Six. Two of those will only entertain when shots are fired at their feet. The least entertaining are men fifty to sixty-four with low incomes and young children.

49. How many years of your life will you spend in the bathroom?

Seven. More, if you are a men's room attendant.

50. If you're a panhandler, who's likelier to come through—someone earning under fifteen thousand dollars or someone earning over fifty thousand?

The former, according to Esquire *magazine, the readers of which you can pretty much write off.*

51. According to a *Times Mirror* survey, do women overestimate the importance of breast size to men?

Yes. Most men don't even think about their breast size.

52. Would more girls like to grow up to be like their fathers, or boys like their mothers?

Boys like their mothers, 71 percent to 65 percent. Just to keep the record straight, 73 percent of the girls would like to grow up to be like their mothers, and 79 percent of boys like their fathers. I must be one of the few who would like to grow up to be like my child.

53. Roper says that the odds against a woman controlling a remote control are what?

   a. *two to one*
   b. *four to one*
   c. *ten to one*

   a. *But wouldn't you forgo the remote and the answering-machine message if you had the checkbook?*

54. Is romance more important to men or women on vacation?

Men, 38 percent to 32 percent. Call us dreamers.

55. How many Americans drink Coke for breakfast?

About a million. Got to wash down the Moon Pie with something.

56. According to *Glamour,* do more women find "nudity" or "nothing" more offensive on TV?

Nudity edges out nothing, 6 percent to 5 percent. I'd like to know where this nudity they're finding turns up. I've only seen it on Wild Kingdom *and* Masterpiece Theatre.

57. What percentage of Americans keep a "watchcat?"

   a. *7 percent*
   b. *16 percent*
   c. *51 percent*

   c. *Over half of cat owners claim they keep it for security reasons, something they might want to rethink should they find her brushing up to a cat burglar.*

• Deep Background:

Do the Chinese Believe in Hell?

Traditional Chinese conceive of hell as a cross between Dante's Inferno and Chicago's city council. The nether world consists of ten courts, each ruled by a king and subdivided into sixteen wards. The king with the most clout is Yen Lo of the Fifth, who, as plenipotentiary of the lower regions, dispatches officers of the court to bring in and book the dead. The book used is the *Book of Destiny,* an unauthorized biography dredging up all the individual's doings from his or her most recent lifetime as well as all previous ones, not exactly a quick read. Where you go from here depends pretty much on how much the judges of hell like your book. The Chinese believe there is a place for everything and in hell everything has its place among the 128 hot hells, 8 cold hells, 8 dark hells, and the 84,000 theme hells designed with you, the sinner, in mind.

According to the folklore, should you notice a large bird-headed thunder god with a hammer in one talon and a chisel in the other at the feeder, you'll probably want to leave a note for the paperboy, and throw a few things in a bag.

58. In Tulsa, 41 percent of the shopping trips to discount stores are motivated by the need for what?

 a. *toiletries*
 b. *children's products*
 c. *entertainment*

 a. *By the time I get to Tulsa, she'll be flossing. Marketers now consider Tulsa to be the most "normal" city in America. If you're "normal," you should be living there.*

59. Are more men or women in favor of genetic engineering?

 Men, 71 percent to 58 percent. More men would genetically engineer women, and more women would genetically engineer men.

60. Who was the greater president, George Washington or Ronald Reagan?

 Washington, but it's close: 25 percent say he was the greatest, to 21 percent for Reagan. History's verdict could, of course, change once it's revealed exactly where Washington slept. (Reagan was easier to pin down in that regard.) For the record: Kennedy came in #1, Lincoln #2, FDR #3, and Truman, Washington, and Reagan were pretty much in a dead heat following. (Harris)

61. Who's richer, agnostics or Episcopalians?

Agnostics, by $300 (probably what they save from the collection plate). The median income for agnostics is $33,300 to an even $33K for Episcopalians. There's only a hundred dollars' difference between a Hindu ($27,800) and a Catholic ($27,700).

62. If you haven't been already, you are most likely to be born on which day of the week?

a. *Tuesday*
b. *Wednesday*
c. *Thursday*

a. *Fewer babies are being born on weekends, for the convenience of physicians. Ours, however, was born exactly at showtime: ten on a Saturday morning.* Whad'ya Know!

63. What is the ratio of women who buy most of their clothes on sale?

a. *nineteen out of twenty*
b. *seven out of eight*
c. *three out of four*

c. *These are* Glamour *readers, who may not be living in Tulsa. Consuela only buys things that have been marked down twice, making them, through natural selection, the most fashion-resistant items of apparel—and, no returns!*

64. Of people who stay up past midnight, which age group is likeliest to be doing housework?

    a. *18–29*
    b. *30–44*
    c. *45–59*

b. *Since I'm leaving that demographic, I'll let you know what happens next.*

65. Do more farmers own Red Wing or Wolverine work boots?

Red Wing, 29.3 percent to 10.1 percent for Wolverine; 7.3 percent for Tingly; Texas Steer 3.6 percent, and Sears 2.4 percent. Birkenstocks: 0.0 percent. (Successful Farming)

66. What percentage of Iowans would like to relive their high school days?

    a. *36 percent*
    b. *51 percent*
    c. *72 percent*

c. *This means that three out of four Iowans either had a great or an awful time in high school. I, personally, would like to go back just to see if my locker combination (33-34-17) still works.*

67. It's not you, it's that one in

    a. *four*
    b. *eight*
    c. *twelve*

people passing on the street is experiencing heartburn.

    c. *So don't take those sour expressions personally.*

68. Is more Jell-O consumed on Saturday or Sunday?

Sunday; it's not even close: 18 percent to 9 percent. You know how it is—on Saturday, you just want to be out, not thinking about Jello-O. I've finally figured out how to get the peaches to suspend, by the way: let harden and insert using a scalpel.

69. One guy in a

    a. *hundred*
    b. *thousand*
    c. *million*

spoons yogurt onto his cereal?

    b. *This, apparently, is driven by a mucus deficit.*

70. Participants in a study watch a tape of a shopper accidentally knocking over a toilet paper display. Given three endings to the incident, which do they prefer?

a. *The shopper flees.*

b. *The shopper, embarrassed, tries to rebuild the pyramid while it continues to topple.*

c. *An idiot comes out and explains he's on* Totally Hidden Video.

b. The study concludes that this is an expression of empathy among klutzes.

71. Women think men are preoccupied with sports, sex, and ogling attractive women. Are they?

No, many don't follow sports at all. When it comes to ogling, you'll be interested to know: 60 percent of women don't think it's a big deal, as long as you (1) don't say a word, and (2) don't move your head, unless you can disguise it as a tic.

72. During the eighties, migraines (among Americans) increased by how much?

a. *30 percent*
b. *60 percent*
c. *75 percent*

b. *Before the eighties, people just thought they had a bad headache. By the end of the nineties, everyone should have a migraine and not be in the mood for a new century at all.*

73. As yuppies slide down the economic ladder, are fewer getting the yuppie flu?

Yes, but more are getting yuppie slivers.

74. A twenty-eight-year-old female who works it in during her lunch hour to the tune of about a hundred dollars is the profile of the average

> a. *aerobics enthusiast*
> b. *call girl*
> c. *shoplifter*

> c. *According to the National Shoplifting Trends Report, which you can rip off at better newsstands everywhere.*

75. Which of the following buzzwords on products has declined the most?

> a. *heart*
> b. *pure*
> c. *fresh*

> a. Heart *(40 percent decline);* pure *(− 23 percent);* fresh *(− 18 percent).* Natural *is up 25 percent, and the prefixes* envi- *and* eco- *are up 21 percent and 10 percent respectively, but* radio- *is going nowhere.*

76. What is the company called that got the brainstorm to ship New York City sludge to Colorado for the winter wheat?

> a. *Enviro-Gro*
> b. *Eco-Natural*
> c. *Crème de la Sludge*

> a. *See?*

77. What was the percentage of farmers who listed their religion as "Jewish" on the *Successful Farming* questionnaire?

a. *3 percent*
b. *.5 percent*
c. *0 percent*

c. *And even fewer are in hogs.*

78. Out of four dog owners, how many say they are as attached to Bowser as they are to their spouses or children?

a. *one*
b. *two*
c. *three*

a. *This is according to the Frosty Paws people, who make ice cream for dogs and nothing for spouses or children.*

79. Does a woman want a gun that looks cute or a gun that looks like a gun?

A gun that looks like a gun, according to Sonny Jones, editor of Women and Guns. *Don't try to sell them a little bunny that spews hollow points.*

• Deep Background:

Who Took the First Bath?

The first bath was taken about 2500 B.C. at Mohenjo-Daro in the Indus valley, the cradle of bathing. While the Hindus bathed religiously, the ancient Egyptians bathed only when the Nile rose, or when held under by the Romans. The Greeks, for their part, not only sported with the gods, they bathed with them afterward; only the patrician upper classes bathed, although the lower classes were allowed to pass water. Modern science was buoyed by a discovery in a bathtub, when Archimedes realized he would have to fill the tub less full or risk losing the cleaning lady.

While the Greeks may have been clean, the Romans had bath complexes which they installed in all conquered provinces in an attempt to make the world safe for a nice soak. Soon, most of the empire boasted hot and cold running aqueducts. According to Plutarch, the changing room at the Baths of Caracalla, with its one hundred thousand lockers, was the eighth wonder of the world.

Surprisingly, in the centuries that followed, bathing did not wash with many Europeans, due to the prevailing attitudes of the Church, which held that bathing was an immodest activity in that it was done naked. As a result, the truly devoted had to make their baptisms last.

---

80. According to the Epcot poll, only one region in the country considers breakfast the most important meal. Which?

Ironically, the only one that serves grits, the South (although only 10 percent of southerners said they actually enjoyed breakfast, so there you go).

81. What percentage of women with best friends don't know if it's a man or a woman?

a. *1 percent*
b. *2 percent*
c. *3 percent*

a. *Eighty-one percent said it was clearly a woman, and 18 percent had no doubt it was a man. Zero percent of men didn't know if their best friend was a man or a woman; 69 percent said it was a man and 31 percent a woman. (Gallup—a man)*

82. Speaking of sex, who's more likely to still be in the nest at age twenty-four—DuWayne or Donna?

DuWayne: 60 percent of males eighteen to twenty-four are living at home—48 percent of females are. Both figures have been on the rise for three decades, indicating that parents are better off leaving home when their kids are eighteen.

83. If you want to live longer, would you be better off being Swedish or Japanese?

Japanese, who have the greatest life expectancy, 79.1 years, to 77.1 for the Swedes. You could gain an extra year and a half if you moved to Canada, but what to do with it?

84. Has evolution led to more males with chest hair or without it?

Nature is ambivalent on this one—it's about even. Darwin had chest hair, though.

85. According to a study at De Paul, how much longer does it take a woman to remember a joke than a man?

> a. *twenty seconds*
> b. *two minutes*
> c. *it'll come to her*

> a. *To be exact, 69.5 seconds to 49.25. This does not include false starts or beginning with the punch line.*

86. According to the Gerber people, what percentage of baby food is consumed by "other than babies"?

> a. *3 percent*
> b. *6 percent*
> c. *13 percent*

> b. *Mostly by Robocop and people who go for that single-serving convenience.*

87. Are more adults interested in religion or VCRs?

> *Religion, you'll be reassured to know, although there may be some who worship VCRs. They certainly work in strange ways.*

88. Once and for all—paper? Or plastic?

> *Paper, 48 percent to 37 percent, even though they snarl at you because they can just dump it in the plastic. According to Gallup, 53 percent of men say "paper," to 43 percent of women, while one in eight asks for both, and 2 percent simply cup their hands.*

89. Given a map with a mileage scale, how many Americans can't figure out how far it is to Sault Ste. Marie?

    a. *one in four*
    b. *one in three*
    c. *one in two*

    b. *The one self-designated as "navigator."*

90. What percentage of Americans do not avoid fat?

    a. *44 percent*
    b. *30 percent*
    c. *19 percent*

    a. *Many, as a result, run smack into it.*

91. Men cry most for what reason?

    a. *for no particular reason, they just feel like it*
    b. *while watching movies or TV*
    c. *over water bills*

    b. *Men and women cry most over men, while women cry for other women over men, or for the release, or for the release of women who are with men, and, rarely, for the release of men.*

92. All right, then, who's more "hands on," women or men?

    Women—but of course, more women have their hands on men, while . . . oh, never mind. It's close enough, 82 percent of women say they are "hands on" kinds of gals, while 80 percent of the guys are always up to something. At least when it's in the garage, you know where they are.

93. Are you more sociable now than you will be in ten years?

Probably, as sociability, the preference for being with other people, declines with age, as you get increasingly tired of both the people you know and people you meet who remind you of them. The most sociable are the sixteen- to nineteen-year-olds (89 percent), who mistakenly find one another interesting.

94. What percentage of eighteen- to twenty-year-olds think the president, when playing Commander in Chief, should wear a uniform?

  a. *.5 percent*
  b. *5 percent*
  c. *15 percent*

  c. *Maybe Everett Koop's old uniform.*

95. What percentage of the American public thinks Congress considers itself above the law?

  a. *75 percent*
  b. *83 percent*
  c. *94 percent*

  b. *And 100 percent of Congress.*

96. What percentage of the American public does not finish what it starts?

    a. *5 percent*
    b. *11 percent*
    c. *31 percent*

    b. *A lot more should never finish what they start, and a good deal more should never have started it in the first place. Some will tell you that, despite appearances, it is finished.*

97. Watching *The Wonder Years* lowers the metabolism of girls, ages seven to eleven, by what percentage?

    a. *14 percent*
    b. *50 percent*
    c. *100 percent*

    a. *Which, according to Tufts, can result in weight gain during the half hour. The control was making seven-year-old girls watch* MacNeil/Lehrer.

98. How many Americans, out of three, would order more ethnic dishes if they knew what the heck was in them?

    Two. The other one already knows. One American in twelve has sampled something they will never have again at the Food Court in the mall.

• Deep Background:

Have All Presidents Had Pets?

Now that the guard has changed from the Bushes' Millie, the pick-of-the-literate spaniel, to the Clintons' cat Socks (reportedly more interested in litter than literature), a glance at history reveals that the White House could as easily have been called Animal House: it has been a rare interlude indeed when the Oval Office has not been littered with rawhide chews, saucers of milk or salt licks. It is said that during the Cuban Missile Crisis, for example, President Kennedy sent for his dog, Charlie, even before summoning his brother Robert. Some revisionist historians go so far as to suggest that Charlie chewed up Khrushchev's provocative message, averting a nuclear confrontation, although this may be overstating his contributions.

Lyndon Johnson was so fond of his three dogs, he ordered that they ride in the presidential limousine while Hubert Humphrey ran alongside. Johnson believed his beagles liked being suspended by their ears, an early indicator of problems with presidential style to come. Lincoln, Harding, Coolidge (who also kept a battalion of cats), and both Roosevelts often sought the company of furry friends during times of crisis; Nixon, who had more than a few such times, permanently stationed his Irish setter, King Timahoe, in his room, relieving Pat of that particular watch. Franklin Roosevelt's dog, Fala, was the first dog to be inducted into the army, rising to the rank of private, while Harding's Laddie Boy had his own chair at Cabinet meetings and has a monument in Washington, D.C.—something that cannot be said of his master.

There have been exotic pets in the presidential menagerie as well, including Hoover's alligators, Wilson's sheep, and Jackson's parrot, Poor Poll, which, at his funeral, unleashed a stream of obscenities recognized by many of the three thousand assembled as the very sentiments of Old Hickory. The bird was removed in the midst of what many thought to be the most fitting eulogy of the day.

---

99. If you want Willard Scott to say hello to you when you're one hundred, you had better move to where?

    a. *Hawaii*
    b. *Kansas*
    c. *Iowa*

a. *If Willard doesn't live to be at least a hundred, a lot of us are going to be disappointed.*

100. When listening to peppy music, do you eat peppy?

Yes, an average of 5.1 more bites per minute, compared to the very same meal eaten in an elevator. (Johns Hopkins study)

101. Do more Americans have bowling balls or obese dogs?

Obese dogs—20.2 million to 19 million bowling balls. And more and more Americans have dogs that look like bowling balls.

102. You are the average American. Have you put on a little weight?

Yes. According to Harris (who doesn't look like he's been starving)—those Americans classifiable as overweight have increased from 58 percent of the population in 1983 to 64 percent now. It appears that we will never be one nation under weight.

103. What percentage of Americans are members of at least one minority group?

All of us, according to American Demographics, *although suspicions remain that some have joined minority groups just for the food. Many Americans—a majority in fact—belong to several minority groups, and have great difficulty in finding a hat that looks good on them.*

104. Do young people between the ages of twelve and seventeen spend less time at cultural events or thinking?

Cultural events, which rate a full eighteen minutes per week, compared to forty-eight minutes thinking (a full six commercial breaks). This last figure obviously does not include time spent thinking about the opposite sex—it's just surprising there are forty-eight minutes a day left over. The American use of Time Project also finds this age group spends very little time writing letters, doing yard work, taking naps, or caring for adults.

105. I weigh 176 pounds. All right, 178. I could not work as a flight attendant on which of the following airlines?

    a. *United*
    b. *Delta*
    c. *American*

    a. *It's no guarantee that I could get the job, but I could still put on ten (all right, eight) pounds and have a shot at Delta and American.*

106. When showing affection toward, hopefully, someone deserving of it, is the term of endearment used more likely to be *baby* or *pumpkin?*

    I don't know what they're calling each other out in the patch, but indoors, 5.4 percent say baby, *while 4.6 percent find something about* squash *appealing; 26.4 percent use* honey *to everyone except feminists; 4.7 percent, if you let them, will call you* sweetheart; *and 6.1 percent will go so far as to use your name, memory permitting. (Korbel survey)*

107. What do lawyers hate most about lawyers?

> a. *they remind them of themselves*
> b. *greed*
> c. *obnoxiousness*

> c. *And 56 percent cite it in a loud, annoying fashion, while 34 percent say it's conceit; 26 percent greed; 24 percent inflexibility; and 21 percent "their ties."*

108. If you were the anti-Cupid and wanted to shoot an arrow into the air with the least chance of hitting a couple having sex, which night should you draw back your bow?

> *Tuesday, according to* Working Mother. *Wednesday, of course, is hump day.*

109. Butter buyers, I'll tell you right now, are more likely to listen to classical radio. But how much more likely are they to?

> a. *35 percent*
> b. *50 percent*
> c. *67 percent*

> a. *This would suggest a correlation between butterfat content and public radio. More Americans with advanced degrees buy butter, which is something the dairy boys should play up.*

110. One of

> a. *twenty-five*
> b. *ten*
> c. *five*

people who pass on the street are cohabiting.

> a. *Your job: find out who, and warn them what it can lead to.*

111. Do more baby boomers plan to seek out "more and better friendships" or "shop for bargains"?

> *Wrong—"more and better friendships," particularly the ones that can do you some good, 55 percent to 47 percent. (Gallup)*

112. Verily, even as we speaketh, are more people reading the Good Book or a "how to" book?

> *"How to," 5 percent to 2 percent. But, friends, isn't the Bible really a "how to" book? Friends?*

113. Speaking of the Good Book, the Bible is the book corporate CEOs and college presidents (same guys, in many cases) recommend as a first read. What's second?

> a. Catcher in the Rye
> b. Up the Establishment
> c. My Darling, My Hamburger

> a. *Beneath that Brooks Brothers exterior beats the heart of Holden Caulfield.*

114. Would more wives like to fix their husbands' personal habits or temper?

> *Well, it's close, but you knew it had to be personal habits (23 percent to 21 percent). (It's 100 percent of my*

wife.) Women take the fact that a man stays pretty much intact after they marry as a personal affront. Then it's salary (20 percent); his family (17 percent); his hobbies (10 percent); and his friends (7 percent). Oh, and another thing . . .

115. How many Americans in five care for household plants?

One. The other four may care for them, but they don't water them or polish their leaves. A very small percentage is openly hostile to household plants, purposely overwatering or introducing household solvents into their pots. Statistically, if you are fifty-eight, married, and a female living in the Northeast, you must care for a houseplant.

116. Are department store shoppers more willing to pay extra for places to sit or restrooms?

Despite some overlapping here, shoppers vote for more restrooms—and in the store, not across the International Food Court Mall and down the corridor next to the Tattoos and Ears Pierced Parlor. Moreover, 43 percent want refunds at any time; 31 percent, in-store baby-sitting; and 12 percent, valet parking. And throw in that Steuben glass, would you?

117. When dining with a member of the opposite sex for the first time, who eats less: men, women, or men and women?

Men and women, according to a study at the University of Toronto, which concludes that women want to be seen as "feminine" by picking at their plates, while men are trying to avoid the gas that will become the hallmark of any long-term relationship.

118. According to Domino's Pizza drivers, do women with rollers in their hair tip better or worse than women without?

Better, and both tip better than men, with or without rollers in their hair. Most people, by the way, not just you, answer the door shoeless.

119. Do more people believe you shouldn't "count your chickens before they hatch," or you shouldn't "cry over spilt milk"?

The former, 93 percent to 88 percent. There is a certain segment of the population which, while it wouldn't dream of counting an unhatched chicken, still cry when they spill milk. The 13 percent who insist on putting all their eggs in one basket are aphorism resistant. (Bruskin)

120. Among people who said they would be celibate for life "if the money were right," what was the going price?

a. *one million*
b. *four to five million*
c. *ten million, and a bonus for signing*

b. *Then they go and marry and do it for nothing.*

121. Out of the six people in your carpool van, how many are carsick?

> *Two. One's heartsick, one's homesick, and one doesn't know when to shut up. That leaves you.*

122. What percentage of schoolchildren say they try to trade or throw away the fruit in their lunches?

> a. *5 percent*
> b. *45 percent*
> c. *95 percent*

> a. *Seventy-seven percent claim they eat it, leaving 18 percent of fruit unaccounted for. A cubbyhole check may be in order.*

123. Do dog owners seek medical attention (for themselves)

> a. *20 percent more often*
> b. *20 percent less often*
> c. *as often as*

cat owners?

> b. *When sick as a dog, dog owners will bring their dogs in. Cat owners will seek medical attention for the slightest fur ball.*

124. American children six to fourteen years of age have

> a. *six billion dollars*
> b. *eight billion dollars*
> c. *ten billion dollars*

in small change.

> a. *And yet you never see one pick up a check.*

Places

THEY SAY TRAVEL IS BROADENING, but staying in one place seems to work for me. I don't know, do all those retirees spending their children's inheritance from Winnebagos with folding chairs strapped on back (I know because I drove for twelve miles behind them through Yosemite and it took sixty-five minutes) really come away as *Ubermensch* and *Uberfrau,* or are they just in it for the decals? Me, I like the little metal souvenirs, like my four-inch Eiffel Tower (twenty francs at that) and my thimble from Harrisburg, PA, with the seal on it. It's pretty much conclusive evidence that you've been there, although I do have an assortment of garter-snake-embellished paraphernalia from Inwood, Manitoba—the Garter Snake Capital of the World—

without once having set foot in the snake pits, but, in spring, it's no longer what my fancy turns to.

As kids, we were forced by my dad, who wanted to be known as the "education father," to take educational vacations. At one time I knew how much water it took to raise a ship thirteen feet in the Sault locks, and what Old Ironsides was doing in Boston Harbor. But we drove right past Wall Drugs every time, so I can't claim to be well rounded: the only jackalopes I've seen have been artists' re-creations.

I always regretted not doing what my brother Howard did, traveling single throughout Europe when sex was still recreational. Howard prided himself on a chameleon-like ability to blend into any leaf he lighted upon, although he never went to Iceland, where it's unlikely anyone would mistakenly call out *Lars!* from the train platform. Only last year did I finally make it to Europe with my wife, who brought the wrong shoes for France (and kept getting hobbled by the cobbles and stepping, open-toed, into the dog doo of Paris), got her first wracking cough and fever ("for forever") in Cannes, and, being six months pregnant, had to be pulled up every scenic vista in Barcelona, the hills being thought by many to be the charm of the place. (On the upside, Gaudi's unfinished cathedral made me feel much better about the recreation room.) And speaking of France, well, you've got to love a place where, from every niche, *liberté, fraternité,* and *égalité* let their robes fall open to their waists, particularly when you're traveling with *finalité.* Same thing with the Spanish—the Prado, filled with stern-looking guys in steel hats and corrugated ruffs interspersed with nudes so realistic you could swear they were showing no interest in you. Here, of course, it's possible to take a snapshot of your spouse with a nice Velázquez nymph in the background, and edit the frame later.

So, yes, I guess it is broadening.

---

1. Where can you find a replica of Barbara Mandrell's bedroom?

Why, at Barbara Mandrell Country in Nashville, of course. ($6.50 for adults, living room included.) If you've been to Barbara Mandrell's real bedroom, you're going to think you're dreaming.

2. "Hang on Sloopy" is the official rock song of which state?

Ohio. The McCoys, who immortalized Sloopy, found her in a very bad part of Dayton.

3. True or false? Sushi is hawked in the stands at Three Rivers Stadium in Pittsburgh.

False. Baseball fans have to go all the way to Anaheim to get it, along with yakitori—chicken on a stick—and yakisoba, Chinese spaghetti. In Anaheim, they do the wave just to get the air moving.

4. What do they get for a bag of leaves in Palm Beach?

Up to twelve dollars for the best-selling oak and maple, for that "northern atmosphere" in decorative place settings. And we're just leaving all that atmosphere on the curb.

5. According to the L.A. dress code for cabbies, drivers may not have more than how many shirt buttons undone?

    a. *one*
    b. *two*
    c. *three*

    b. *It doesn't say which two, though. Also: no bold prints or plaids; shirts must be tucked in; and absolutely no shorts, sandals, or sweat suits. The ones in knee-high thongs, leather corsets, and tricolor plumage are the passengers.*

6. The "person access chamber" is the nonsexist term in Sacramento for what common piece of city property?

    The manhole.

7. What's destroying the vinyl boat seats of Kissimmee, Florida?

    a. *vultures*
    b. *walking catfish*
    c. *Hank Gottlieb, who hates boaters with a passion*

    a. *They also eat screens and shingles, and have been known to carry off lawn jockeys.*

8. What is the most expensive city on earth?

    a. *Jersey City*
    b. *Tokyo*
    c. *Tehran*

c. *Twice as costly as New York, and without the Rockettes. Tokyo is #2, Osaka #3, Taipei #4, while Beijing and New York City are lucky to be tied for fifth.*

9. Which World Cup soccer team was ordered not to have sex during the playoffs, Brazil or Italy?

Italy. The Brazilian coach couldn't believe it either. There remains a lot of controversy as to whether you should have World Cup soccer the night before you compete in sex.

10. What percentage of Iowans caught some rays during the past year?

    a. *3 percent*
    b. *26 percent*
    c. *49 percent*

b. The rest just pinked-up their left arms, from here to here, on their twelve-minute commutes to Cedar Rapids.

11. Are more dogs in Los Angeles named Madonna or Big Foot?

Big Foot, twenty-six to eighteen. Forty-nine dogs are named Elvis; ten go by Lady Di; and three (with big floppy ears) answer to Prince Charles.

12. Was Pluto, West Virginia, named for the god of the dead or the dog of the mouse?

The god of the dead, according to the burial chamber of commerce.

13. According to a health survey, Wisconsin, North and South Dakota, Indiana, Michigan, Kentucky, and West Virginia could together be called the "——— States of America."

"Fat." I wouldn't say it to our chubby little faces, though. Twenty-five percent of the residents of these states are classified as "obese."

14. When visiting friends in Russia, is it polite to lounge about in pajamas and ask how much money they make?

Yes—they'd be hurt if you didn't. By the way, if you want shower curtains, you'd better bring them.

15. What percentage of Allied moving vans are headed out of North Dakota?

Seventy percent—North Dakota is the leading producer of outward-bound moving vehicles in the United States. Washington, D.C., led in insies, at least until the Democrats came up with a winning ticket.

16. According to *The Lifestyle Market Analyst,* who follows fashion more, people in New York City or Durango, Colorado?

This is a tough one—the answer is New York City, despite the fact that many New Yorkers tend to dress as if they lived in Durango.

17. Out of the twenty-five thousand men attending the recent marriage fair in Bihar, India, how many lucked out?

Twenty thousand. The other five thousand got married.
Among the Brahmin, it is considered good luck not to meet
the bride until the wedding.

18. Do Californians spend more or less time than average
Americans washing and grooming themselves?

Less—twenty-one minutes to twenty-five minutes nation-
ally. The rule of thumb is the more you commute, the less
you groom, although in Los Angeles, it's still possible to do
both and phone ahead for a nail appointment without leav-
ing the Santa Monica freeway.

19. How many people in Clark County, Georgia, traded in
their randomly assigned *FAT* license plates?

Sixty-five out of ninety. One woman lost forty pounds.

20. You think you're under a lot of pressure on Earth—
how much would you be under on Venus?

Ninety-two times as much. You would end up smaller but
lighter, since the gravity is 90 percent of Earth's.

21. There are, according to the license plates, ten thousand
lakes in Minnesota. How many are there back home in
Finland?

They have 187,888. A better question would be, Where's
the land in Finland? (We know where the fins are; they're
in the 187,888 lakes.)

• Deep Background:

Is That Story About the Foreign Student Who Passed Out on the Floor of the Disco True?

The foreign student, the salami, and the friend who's an emergency room nurse and saw it are all elements in one American folk legend, or urban myth, a body of lore so improbable, people take it for the gospel. They include the woman bitten by an exotic snake concealed in the lining of her fur coat; the dead grandma in the station wagon; the cement poured in the Corvette/Porsche/Lamborghini; the seventy-five-dollar Corvette/Porsche/Lamborghini; the Buick loaded with options, including a dead mafioso in the trunk; the stolen suitcase containing a dead dog; the naked traveler accidentally dumped out the back door of his camper; the disembodied hook left dangling from the window of the car parked on lover's lane; the black widow spider in the beehive/dreadlocks/spike hairdo; the naked lady and the meter reader; the Volkswagen and the pachyderm; the parakeet and the vacuum cleaner; the cat in the microwave; the fish in the trunk; and the alligators in the sewers.

Nor is there anything to what you heard about Richard Gere or Jamie Lee Curtis.

22. The residents of which of the following cities walk the fastest?

    a. *Fresno, California*
    b. *Bronx, New York*
    c. *Springfield, Massachusetts*

c. *A typical resident of Springfield rifles across sixty feet of sidewalk in 11.1 seconds, a full 3.6 seconds faster than a Fresnan, making Springfield the fastest of thirty-six cities tested.*

23. Underscoring the contention of many that "English cuisine" is an oxymoron, what, exactly, are "battered trotters"?

Sheep's feet, especially good in months with s in them. They are simmered in broth, battered, and trotted out.

24. You're looking at a small lot in Tokyo. What's the most it could cost you?

Eighty-eight thousand dollars per square meter, not bad considering that's 10.76 square feet (the going rate in the Ginza).

25. In the South, what have you got if you cream together oleo and sugar, add flour, and roll out the dough about one-half-inch thick, cut out circles with the lid of a fruit jar, and bake in a greased pan for twenty minutes?

Shortnin' bread. You supply mammy's little baby.

26. According to the dog-and-cat census, there are, officially, how many cats in Marquette, Michigan, in the Upper Peninsula?

Nine. Apparently not all the felines answered the door.

27. Mexico City finally has one; is it a Ronald McDonald House or a Leon Trotsky House?

The latter, some fifty years after he was mistaken for a block of ice. Trotsky Houses have not shown any sign of catching on elsewhere.

28. According to the Italian Association for Demographic Studies, who cheats more, Italian husbands or wives?

According to a poll of twenty thousand adults, wives, 66 percent to 32 percent. While Papa's out pinching in the palazzo, Mama, she's a making pasta.

29. Believed to be the most heavily sedated city in the world, some 62 percent of its population use sleeping pills due to street noise. Which city is it?

    a. *Rome*
    b. *Cairo*
    c. *Athens*

    b. *The Sphinx hasn't shut its eyes in five thousand years.*

30. You now can be fined for cruising McHenry Avenue in the heart of the onetime "scoop the loop" capital of America. Where is it?

Modesto, California, locale of American Graffiti. *If you pass the same cop three times, you have to do a shotgun.*

31. How long can you wait for a dial tone in Argentina?

    a. *three minutes/local call, one hour/long distance*
    b. *ten minutes/local, all day/long distance*
    c. *you have to go to Uruguay for a dial tone*

    b. *For a few australs, however, you can hire someone to wait for your dial tone.*

32. Culturally speaking, which rates higher: Newark or Minneapolis/St. Paul?

Newark, New Jersey, according to the Places Rated Almanac, *ranks #8 in cultural amenities (museums, opera, theater, dance, and, for some reason, public radio), hard on the heels of San Francisco, and hard on the toes of Cleveland (#9) and Minneapolis/St. Paul (#10). The Twin Cities remain the only place in the Midwest where you have to dress, however.*

33. Grease wrestling is the national sport of

Turkey. And Turk wrestling . . .

34. Out West, what does a cowboy mean by "Mormon dip"?

Gravy.

35. A Milwaukeean says he'll "come by the house later." Does that mean he'll stop?

> *Yes. he might even come in, if you let him. Newcomers, hearing the phrase, often erroneously assume an offer to purchase is imminent.*

36. A family of

    a. *four*
    b. *eight*
    c. *twenty-six*

could go to the movies in Mexico City for the price of one in Tokyo.

> c. *On the other hand, baby-sitters are for life in Japan.*

37. Des Moines ranks number one in per capita consumption of which of the following?

    a. *Skippy peanut butter*
    b. *Jell-O*
    c. *Kraft macaroni*

> b. *For some reason, they're going with the generic macaroni. With the tuna mixed in, you can't really tell, anyway.*

38. How many Britons are first-rate eccentrics?

a. *one in ten thousand*
b. *one in one thousand*
c. *one in ten*

a. *Seems higher, though, doesn't it? Maybe it's just that a man who dresses as a pink elephant and rappels down office towers gets an inordinate amount of press.*

39. In the rural Midwest, what does the expression "to cut one's foot" mean?

To step in manure, according to farm reporter Max Armstrong of WGN radio.

40. Which, according to Survey Sampling, Inc., is the most sampled community in the United States?

a. *Des Moines, Iowa*
b. *Peoria, Illinois*
c. *Midland, Texas*

c. *The runners-up: Portland, Oregon; Boulder, Colorado; and Grand Forks, North Dakota. Folks in Midland have been polled so often, they feel like Herefords.*

41. What now stands in Chicago on the spot where Mrs. O'Leary's cow kicked over the lantern?

a. *the American Dairy Association*
b. *Mrs. O'Leary's lawyer*
c. *the Chicago Fire Academy*

c. *Nice touch, don't you think? The only thing that didn't burn in the Great Fire was the pumping station and the Cubs. You couldn't set fire to the Cubs.*

42. What does the Arabian expression "Better a handful of dates than to own the Gate of Peacocks and be kicked in the eye by a broody camel" mean?

> *Pretty much what it says, although it sounds like sour dates. Ideally, a guy could own the Gate of Peacocks and not be kicked in the eye by a broody camel. (Broody camels, by the way, are merely suffering from water retention.)*

• Deep Background:

Why Is There No Panacea?

A panacea is a remedy for all disease or for the ills of the world; a cure-all. There can be no panacea, because were one found, the big drug companies would sit on it. The term itself comes from the Greek goddess of healing, of whom Plutarch is said to have offhandedly remarked, "Panacea is good for what ails you."

In his quest for relief from the suffering other than that which he himself inflicts, man has left no stone unturned, including the bezoar, a medicinal stone found only in the dung of a particular species of goat, the *pazan,* indigenous to the West Indies. The annals of science do not record when this particular leap of faith was made, or by whom, but Samuel Johnson, in his dictionary, notes that the stone was "good for

gout, rickets, hysteria, diabetes, varicose veins, smallpox, di-
lated stomach, afflictions of the spleen, and malposition of
the pelvic organs." Swallowing a bezoar was thought to be
an antidote for poisoning, proving that not only are there no
panaceas, but the cure is often worse than the disease.

---

43. Which bothers Iowans the most: the heat or the
humidity?

> *No question, the humidity, 87 percent to 6 percent. Come
> to Des Moines in August, and you'll know why there's no
> expression, "It's the heat."* (Iowa Poll, Des Moines
> Register)

44. If a Japanese is making *ibiki wo kaku,* is he

  a. *snoring*
  b. *fileting blowfish*
  c. *singing along with a cassette in a nightclub?*

  a. *Snoring. This is what snoring sounds like in Japanese.*

45. Wadsworth, Ohio, is associated with what "throw"?

  a. *toilet*
  b. *bull*
  c. *cow chip*

  a. *The Great Wadsworth Toilet Toss (June, see your* Rand
  McNally Travel Guide), *where a good toss of a forty-two-
  pound toilet is around twenty-seven feet. The secret: "Just*

make sure the rim's clean." The proceeds, by the way, go
to kidney research.

46. What's a "Calgary Redeye"?

*A drink consisting of half beer and half tomato juice. This,
depending on your point of view, either ruins the beer or
ruins the tomato juice.*

47. The world's largest and oldest organism was recently
discovered in Michigan's Upper Peninsula. What is it?

*A ten-thousand-year-old thirty-seven-acre fungus, poised, I
might add, right on the Wisconsin border. You've got to
feel bad for the guy who bought the forty acres for his cabin,
and now keeps bringing up spores on the perk test.*

48. When it comes to taking medicine, the English prefer
tablets, and the Germans lean toward injections. How do the
French take it?

*In the south, via suppositories. A knottier problem for the
European Community than resolving the gauge of train
tracks.*

49. In Nigeria, is it friendly to be addressed as "my friend"?

No. According to The African Guardian, *"my friend" is
a "stupid, despicable fellow." Ah, you've met my friend.*

50. True or false? You need a permit to move to or from
East Orange, New Jersey.

True; ostensibly to distinguish movers from thieves. It's easy to tell a mover from a burglar, really: the thieves don't break anything.

51. According to Hunter S. Thompson, "Hell is a viciously overcrowded version" of what city?

    a. *Phoenix*
    b. *Las Vegas*
    c. *Fargo*

    a. *The truth is, Phoenix is getting crowded, too.*

52. What's the biggest the dirty words on your bumper sticker can be in Louisiana?

    a. *six inches*
    b. *half an inch*
    c. *one eighth of an inch*

    c. *This can only serve to increase tailgating among the myopic.*

53. The high-speed magnetic trains developed in Germany may soon take Scandinavians to Mecca and Los Angelenos to where?

    Vegas, at 310 miles per hour, although the trip back may seem a lot slower. And to the Swedes, coming back from Mecca.

54. If you're the type of tourist who hates missing any opportunity to view famous human parts on display, what treat have you got in store for yourself in Northfield, Minnesota?

The purported ear of Charlie Pitts, one of Jesse James's boys, left behind in the Northfield raid. Looks kind of like a bat.

55. According to the London *Times,* how many English kids skip school each day to play amusement devices?

One hundred thousand, and the Times *is not amused.*

56. Was Napoleon, North Dakota, named after the guy with his hand in his tunic, or one of the early real-estate developers?

The man with his hand in your tunic, realtor Napoleon Goodsill.

57. When you think of four green flying pigs, you naturally think of what?

Cincinnati, where the bronze pigs adorn a new monument honoring the city's past fame as "Porkopolis."

58. True or false? Idaho's state song is "Here We Have Idaho."

True.

59. Was the longest vegetable in Wales a cucumber or a parsnip?

Not even close—a parsnip, eighty-nine inches to cucumber, thirty-four. It's impossible to get small vegetables in Wales, where one cocktail onion can displace your entire martini.

60. How many Dutch cows pass through Amsterdam airport each year?

    a. *are you kidding?*
    b. *one pair (sisters)*
    c. *ten thousand*

    c. *What's worse, they fly standby. And it doesn't end there: seventeen hundred horses, five hundred tons of tropical fish, and two million chickens could make you forget entirely about those two annoying kids behind you.*

61. If a friend says, "Let's have dinner in Madrid," what time should you be there?

You probably want to pick up the sitter around ten o'clock, hoping that she hasn't done too much tapas *hopping, because Madrileños like to eat between ten and midnight. Well, when you take a three-hour siesta in the afternoon, and work until eight, things get pushed back a little. A better question is, "Where are they during their siestas?"*

62. What are *tapas?*

Tapas *are what they'll be playing for you, fellow traveler, if you empty enough of the little happy-hours dishes of appetizers, like marinated mussels, sautéed squid, casseroles that look nothing like any dish you might have brought to pass, and a few slices of* jamón Serrano. *Then you're ready to seek out your entrée: hake with baby eels (they look up at you).*

63. Given an Oreo, what do the Japanese do?

   a. *eat just the cookie part*
   b. *eat just the filling*
   c. *have no part*

   a. *In fact, Yamazaki Nabisco sells 'em without the filling (which the Japanese consider too sweet). My wife scrapes the white stuff into the sink, where it forms an excellent barrier against any moisture escaping. Me, I eat the whole darn thing, and have taught my daughter to do the same.*

64. Are the Chinese authorities trying to stamp out

   a. *mah-jongg*
   b. *ancestor worship*
   c. *Western music*

   a. *Introduced by middle-aged Hadassah ladies, mah-jongg has so captivated the Chinese people that many lose their wives in the game, using their spouses as unsecured collateral.*

65. What is the biggest problem faced by the twenty-foot Holstein cow statue that stands at the gates of Plymouth, Wisconsin?

   a. *hunters mistake it for a twenty-foot deer*
   b. *pranksters continually pull her four-foot teats off*
   c. *Hindus on pilgrimage have been clogging up highway*

   b. *They just replaced her again, but a lot of people think this one looks more like a Dalmatian.*

66. What does Moscow's first sex shop feature, along with the usual inflatables and Taiwanese aids?

a. *Doan's pills—thought to be an aphrodisiac*
b. *Tampons*
c. *Silly Putty*

b. *I don't know—maybe party favors?*

67. In Indiana, baby chicks outnumber Hoosiers

    a. *ten to one*
    b. *twenty to one*
    c. *one hundred to one*

    a. *Fifty-six million chicks. You figure out the number of Hoosiers.*

68. If a Russian peasant spits three times, he

    a. *probably is trying to get the taste of bootleg vodka out of his mouth*
    b. *just passed Raisa Gorbachev*
    c. *just passed a cleric*

    c. *This predates Communist rule, by the way, being an old Russian way of saying, "Top o' the morning, Father."*

69. How many checkouts do they have at the Hypermart outside Garland, Texas?

    a. *four—including one express*
    b. *fifty-eight*
    c. *ninety, but only three are open*

    b. *Just the thought of a Hypermart makes me nervous.*

70. According to *Money* magazine, is there any place worse than Flint, Michigan?

Yes, Benton Harbor.

71. In addition to his thirty-six dollars per month, how much does a Saudi *sayyaf*—"swordsman executioner"—get per head?

    a. *$13*
    b. *$33*
    c. *$133*

    c. *The tip (1,500 riyals) comes from the customer, adding insult to serious injury. A beheader does not shake your hand to gauge your weight, but may loosen your tie just to make you comfy.*

72. According to *Maclean's* magazine, what percentage of Canadians think Americans are "aggressive, obnoxious, pig-headed snobs"?

    a. *none*
    b. *29 percent*
    c. *17 percent*

    b. *If this ever comes out, it might affect the 43 percent of us who think Canadians are "friendly, good neighbors."*

73. Does Boston have a street filled with kosher butcher shops, as depicted in *Field of Dreams*?

No, you could plotz before you'll find a kosher chicken in Boston. Try Brookline.

74. How many pages of Andersons are there in the Minneapolis phone book?

    a. *twenty-one*
    b. *thirty-four*
    c. *sixty-eight*

    a. *Surprisingly few.*

75. While we're on the subject, the Kensington rune stone proves that before there were Scandinavians in Minnesota, there were what?

    Scandinavians. In 1898 Olaf Ohman discovered this historical record of eight Swedes and twenty-two Norwegians who passed through in 1362 looking for the Andersons.

76. Out of three residents, how many think a Grand Prix through the streets of Des Moines is a good thing?

    Two, according to the Iowa Poll of the Des Moines Register. *The other one is thinking about crossing the streets of Des Moines.*

77. Thanks to the fall of communism, Hungarians can once again see the what of Saint Stephan?

    a. *head*
    b. *hand*
    c. *ear*

    b. *The holy right hand, in its glass casket, was under lock and key during the former regime. It is not known if more parts will eventually surface, possibly in Northfield, Minnesota.*

78. In the hills and hollers of Missouri, what is "greens and pot licker"?

Greens—mustard, dandelion, lamb's-quarter, cress, poke-boiled with "side meat"—what have you.

79. A Texan seeking one divorce could afford how many in Idaho for the same price?

a. *four*
b. *a dozen*
c. *twenty-nine*

c. *Average of $27,333 for a good ol' Texas divorce lawyer; $950 for the very same service in Idaho.*

80. During the eighties, migraines among Americans increased

a. *30 percent*
b. *60 percent*
c. *75 percent*

b. *Before the eighties, people just thought they had bad headaches. (But when they stretch into the nineties, you know something's wrong.)*

81. There are

    a. *no*
    b. *two*
    c. *eighteen*

Bigfoots living in Ohio.

    c. *Three just around Cleveland (in the Heights?), according to the man behind the* Bigfoot Pocket Manual, *Robert Morgan.*

82. Called the "stolen-car capital of the world," in this European nation it is not uncommon to find the police driving stolen cars. Where?

    Poland, where you can find an estimated sixty thousand "like new" Mercedes, Volvos, and Range Rovers on the lot at any given time ("creampuffs") priced to move. J. D. Powers reports they are even beginning to steal American cars.

83. Forty-five percent of North Dakota's energy needs could be met by:

    a. *wind*
    b. *water*
    c. *South Dakota*

    a. *Must be the wind that's blowing all those moving vans out.*

84. Which—if I might inquire—is the most polite city in the United States?

    a. *Los Angeles*
    b. *Chattanooga*
    c. *Cheyenne*

    c. *Where they give out free parking tickets just for saying howdy! If you'd be so kind as to take the polite tour, you might go on to Charleston, Washington, D.C.(!), Portland, Seattle, Mobile, Pensacola, San Diego, Denver, and Pittsburgh.*

85. Where can you see a man make an eight-ton backhoe do the moonwalk?

    a. *in your dreams*
    b. *Phoenix*
    c. *Tulsa*

    b. *Just to rebut that Hunter Thompson crack about being an overcrowded version of Hell: Phoenix is the home of the North American Backhoe Rodeo Championships, where over a hundred of the nation's finest heavy-equipment operators make those suckers dance.*

86. Are there *karaoke* taxis in South Korea?

    No, in hell. They had them in South Korea, but the sing-alongs were deemed too distracting for the drivers.

• Deep Background:

Have There Always Been Taxes?

While historically the line between taxation and outright extortion appears a bit fuzzy, it is safe to say that whether the best of times or the worst of times, they have always been taxing times. Some Bible historians believe that Moses came down from Sinai with a set of tax tables. Reliefs in Egyptian tombs provide little tax relief, as they depict Eternal Revenue officials with adder heads driving herds of taxpayers toward vulture-headed treasury officials. A poem dating to the Chou Dynasty in China pays tribute to the overlord and his tax collectors:

> Big rat
> Big rat
> Do not gobble our millet.

Taxation probably began in the cradle of civilization and will undoubtedly follow it to the grave. Ancient kings—who claimed to be gods on leave—intercepted offerings made to the main office before they were burnt and of no use to anybody. In return, the subjugated were provided with all the benefits of the modern state: incessant warfare, a rigid class system, and public buildings. In Mesopotamia, Egypt, Sumer, India, and China, taxes were collected in kind—in fact, in all kinds: horns, feathers, jewels, grain, wine, fish, oil, sheep, and family members looking for steady work with no chance of advancement as slaves or concubines.

---

87. Do Hyundais fly?

They do in South Korea, where traffic jams get so bad that military helicopters scramble to pluck disabled cars off the highway, karaoke *tapes still blaring.*

88. Is the "friss" a lively Hungarian dance or a Jewish rite of circumcision?

That's bris.

89. Female flight attendants on China's national airlines must be healthy, have good eyesight and

a. *have their feet bound*
b. *take a required course in livestock management*
c. *be virgins*

c. *Needless to say, there is an acute shortage of flight attendants.*

90. Is it called a Danish in Denmark?

No. Wiener broed: *Vienna bread.*

91. The Portuguese use which of the following in lieu of a decimal point?

a. *dollar sign*
b. *smiley face*
c. *asterisk*

a. *This can cause sticker shock to Americans in Lisbon.*

92. In Hollywood, which are referred to as the "flyover states"?

Everything between Los Angeles and New York.

93. What's the biggest problem in selling pizza in China?

a. *the Chinese characters* Pe-Tzo *mean a "decayed or putrified carcass"*
b. *eating curdled milk products disgusts the Chinese*
c. *a slice tends to flop over a chopstick*

b. *If you think of them being curdled milk products, I guess they'd disgust anybody.*

94. Where is the "Beanee Weenee" capital of the world?

a. *Boston, Massachusetts*
b. *Downers Grove, Illinois*
c. *Charlotte, North Carolina*

c. *Charlotte consumed 113 million pounds of Beanee Weenees—the beanees with the weenies right in them—enough, laid end to end, to complete 84 laps of the Charlotte Motor Speedway and make for a monumental hazard. Charlotte can also lay claim to being the "ketchup" and "Spam" capital, but you don't want to sound like you're blowing your own horn.*

95. Is Blagg on the moon or in Nevada?

Blagg is a pock on the man in the moon's nose approximately two miles across.

96. Smuggling gum into Singapore can net you

a. *a $500 fine*
b. *a $1,200 fine and ninety days in the slammer*
c. *a $6,200 fine and up to a year in jail*

c. *Chewing gum has to be declared on customs forms—and I wouldn't just stick it on there either. There is also a fine for not flushing a toilet in Singapore, which you have to applaud.*

97. In the Argentine pampas, is a *zonda* a pair of chaps or a hot wind?

It's a hot wind, likely through a pair of chaps. Also, what a Jewish caballero says: "Oy, what a zonda!"

98. Mexico City has a plan for cleaning up air pollution that has a lot of people scratching their heads and wondering why they didn't think of that. What is it?

Giant fans—one hundred twenty-four-foot fans, which could blow the smog right into Veracruz.

99. The world's largest six-pack in La Crosse, Wisconsin, can hold the equivalent of how many regular six-packs of Old Style?

a. *39,111*
b. *106,004*
c. *Urrp!*

a. *They get a couple of bowling teams together during Octoberfest, and drain it.*

100. Where is perhaps the only place in America in which you can find a ten-mile row of fifteen-foot-tall teacups and saucers along an expressway?

Phoenix. (Take that, Gonzo.) What looks to a lot of people like a stack of giant dirty dishes is, in reality, art.

101. If a grasshopper with the wingspan of small bird is your cup of tea, you should head for

a. *Trinidad*
b. *Costa Rica*
c. *Florida*

a, b, and c. *They're still turning heads, though, only around Plantation, Florida, where Department of Agriculture official Harold Denmark says, "It almost looks like it is not for real. It is, and it does fly."*

102. Do more Britons have intercourse or chat on the phone in the bathtub?

> *I'm surprised you had to ask: chat on the phone, of course. They'd rather ring somebody up, 10 percent to 2 percent, the latter being roughly the same number that take their pets in with them (including rabbits, turtles, and Persian cats).*

103. In New York City, people with car alarms are supposed to leave what plainly visible when they leave their cars?

> *Their phone numbers. Look for signs like* NO RADIO? CALL 397-1429.

• Deep Background:

W h o   W a s   t h e   S k i n n y   G u y   w i t h the   M u s t a c h e   W h o   A l w a y s   W o r e a   H a t   a n d   W a s   i n   A l l   T h o s e   B a d Detective   Movies?

James Gleason, whose Brooklyn accent and side-of-the-mouth delivery made him one of the most widely used supporting actors in Hollywood in films from *Forty Naughty Girls* to *Murder on a Bridle Path*. Gleason is just one of dozens of character actors so familiar they seem to be members of the family, albeit nameless ones, since they lacked star billing. There was Harold Huber, for instance, the greased-back heavy of undetermined ethnicity in Charlie Chan movies; Richard Loo, who played every sadistic Japanese commanding officer known to Hollywood; Frank McHugh, the man they asked for when they needed an Irishman to do double takes; Mike Mazurki, the ex-wrestler whose chiseled bad looks made him a natural for Moose Malloy in *Murder, My Sweet;* Beryl Mercer, the earth mother who in *All Quiet on the Western Front* cautioned Lew Ayres not against bullets but against "all the no-good women out there." There was Mantan "feets do your stuff" Moreland; Barbara Nichols, the archetypical blond floozy; Alan Mowbray, the butler who mastered his masters in *Topper,* and Maria Ouspenskaya, who, as a gypsy, clued Lon Chaney in to the downside of werewolf bites.

Above all, there was Franklin Pangborn, ubiquitous desk clerk, undisputed master of the pince-nez (were they taped on?), and without a doubt, the only man who ever tried to get Ginger Rogers *out* of a hotel room.

---

104. True or false? The fastest growing segment of burglaries in West Palm Beach, Florida, is boutique theft by organized gangs of transvestites.

> *True. And how do you run in those heels? According to police, the cross-dressing criminals are not only professionals, "they know labels."*

105. How many Japanese males does it take to do the housework of one Swedish male?

> a. *three*
> b. *four*
> c. *five*

> c. *There just aren't enough hours in the week for the Swedish male, who puts in eighteen on housework.*

106. According to *Christianity Today,* scientists in Finland, while drilling nine miles into the earth, discovered what?

> a. *hell*
> b. *nougat*
> c. *a huge cache of single socks*

> a. *They knew it was hell because it didn't look anything like Phoenix.*

107. What is the favorite boy's name in Israel?

> a. *Mohammed*
> b. *Moshe*
> c. *George*

> a. *Although Ahmed is creeping up on Moshe, in second.*

108. Can you practice yoga in a public facility in Toccoa, Georgia?

> *Yes, but you cannot use public funds to open up your thousand-petaled lotus (a county board decision).*

109. What state's name derives from an Indian word meaning "one who puts to sleep?"

    a. *Iowa*
    b. *Mississippi*
    c. *Kansas*

    a. *That's all right;* Chicago *means stinking onions.*

110. How long does yak butter keep without refrigeration?

Indefinitely, providing you live at twenty thousand feet, like, say, in Tibet, where fifty-pound blocks sitting on the table test the aphorism, "The butter of the yak is the sweetest smell in the heavens."

111. A magpie on the roof in Macedonia means

    a. *sickness in the family*
    b. *worse, guests are coming*
    c. *droppings in the gutters*

    b. *Guests are coming. Possibly more magpies.*

112. Do Puerto Ricans favor regular or family-size containers?

Regular. According to Luis Leon of Sterling Products: "If you buy the small bottle, you get to visit Walgreens three times a month."

113. Under legislation pending in Boise, not returning library books could get you

    a. *six months in jail*
    b. *a year in jail*
    c. *fourteen years in jail*

    c. *And if you don't return books to the prison library, they make you spend fourteen years in Boise.*

114. Canadians live an average of

    a. *one year*
    b. *two years*
    c. *three years*

longer than Americans.

    a. *Almost worth the drive to Buffalo for supplies.*

115. How many wild Amazon parrots now colonize Los Angeles?

    a. *several hundred*
    b. *a thousand or so*
    c. *ten thousand*

    b. *The destruction of the rain forest has driven many to Bel Air.*

116. In Scotland, is a "but and ben" a two-room cottage or a bed and breakfast?

A two-room cottage, the term meaning "out and in," as in out of one room and into the other.

117.   South Carolina leads the nation in license plate designs with how many different ones?

   a. *17*
   b. *43*
   c. *179*

   c. *The prisoners stamping them out are now eligible for grants from the National Endowment for the Arts, providing the vanity plates don't get too dicey.*

118.   Ideal for earrings and tie tacks, a quarter of a million are sold annually in souvenir shops in Anchorage alone. What is this new Alaskan motherlode?

   Moose nuggets. Some one hundred thousand moose work around the clock to produce a million pounds a day, the incentive being between $1.25 and $3.00 for each.

119.   The Bismarck, North Dakota, municipal airport has

   a. *two*
   b. *four*
   c. *six*

overcoats to lend visitors unprepared for subzero weather.

   c. *You probably want to bring one along anyway—or leave one, if you can spare it.*

120. What state requires environmentally correct leaf blowers?

Too easy—California, of course, where you have to put a catalytic converter on your leaf blower. Rakes remain unregulated.

• Deep Background:

Is There a Social Register?

Yes, and if you have to ask, you're obviously not in it. It is *The Social Register,* the "Old Money Testament," the same one invented by New Jersey gentleman farmer Louis Keller in 1877, and, in fact, the original "little black book," at 4¾ by 6¼ inches. *The Register* is not so little anymore, either in dimensions (8¾ inches square) or in thickness, due to the fact that a good deal of new money has gotten older since its inception. But you still get lots of blue blood on orange paper.

The easiest way of making *The Social Register* is still the old-fashioned way: well birth. *The Register* will then track your progress through nothing-but-the-best for life, major social gaffes notwithstanding. You can't always tell what those might be: Charles Alden Black got dumped for marrying Shirley Temple; Marcos bosom buddy Doris Duke, Barbara Hutton, and Gloria Vanderbilt were all jettisoned after divorcing; while Ann Eden Crowell shot and killed her husband and stayed in. It's a judgment call.

If you're a climber, you need somebody on the inside ("a subscriber") to write you a letter of recommendation, and, if your lineage, affiliations, spouse, and memberships are up to snuff, you will receive an application to be supported by five more subscribers. Should *The Social Register'*s advisory board give you the pinkies up, you will not only be included in the next edition, but have a chance to buy it for thirty-five dollars.

---

121. In Castile, Spain, must the bride dance the knife-impaled apple dance with every man who puts a coin in the apple?

> *Yes. That's what I call doing the* manzana. *If she drops a coin, he gets it back; otherwise, it's earning a dowry the tough way.*

122. If you order a *calapranzi* in Italy, what are you ordering?

> a. *prawns in white wine and bread crumbs*
> b. *goat intestine stuffed with most of the major organs*
> c. *a dumbwaiter*

> c. *Better check the dictionary—you were probably trying to order a calabrone* (hornet).

123. Pronounce "Leicestershire."

No, that's "Worcestershire."

124. Salisbury steak was discovered in

    a. *Cleveland*
    b. *Leipzig*
    c. *Salisbury, silly*

a. Before then, it was just considered to be hamburger hiding in gravy. Cleveland, by the way, also brought us Life Savers, Muzak, Superman, Day-Glo, steering wheels, Ready-Mix, and the United Way.

125. If you're "in Morocco" in England, you're what?

Bound in leather, or, naked. Starkers, if you please, or "all face," "bare poles," "skuddy," "on the shallows," "in cuerpo," or "wearing your Sunday suit," if you don't please.

Things You Should Have Learned in School

(Had You Been Paying Attention)

● **SOMEWHERE AROUND PUBERTY,** I started hating school. I think it was because some of the biggest potential jerks began to realize their potential, and, overnight, you had to be really nice to them. True, I was equipped for verbal warfare, but that only goes as far as your nose on a junior high school playground, which is why I made friends with Dana, the toughest girl at Steuben Junior High School. She was big, bad, and beautiful, especially if you liked white lipstick and teased hair (I did, on her). Dana and her friends once walked into a party I was at in somebody's basement and put "Sex Machine" on the record player after giving "Meet the Beatles" the old *Blackboard Jungle* toss. I defended her in Mr. Hinz's class when she was put on mock trial for crimes against social studies. She was found guilty, but that just enhanced her reputation, which she appreciated, as she did the strong case I made for living free and carrying a sharp metal teasing comb. I was proud to be her mouthpiece, because Dana had something I could only dream of: overt disregard for authority and an undisguised disdain for the learning environment. True, I looked like a junior accountant in my white shirt, turtleneck dickies, and black Sta-Pressed pants, but inside those black penny loafers walked a rebel without the claws.

Dana had those.

---

1. Should you seek to diligently inquire or to inquire diligently?

You're better off not doing either (it'll come back to haunt you). At the very best you'll end up splitting your infinitive.

2. If you've got an epicarp, a mesocarp, and an endocarp, what are you?

A carp, hey? Back in your seats, just kidding. You're a nice piece of fruit.

3. Speaking of fruit, pick the sense out of the following verse:

Cherry-ripe, ripe, ripe, I cry,
Full and fair ones, come and buy:
If so be, you ask me where they do grow?

I answer there, where my Julia's lips do smile;
There's the land, or cherry-isle.

Robert Herrick, 1648

Obviously, a man who likes produce. You remember Herrick; he was the cleric who wanted to be a flea in another verse, so he could bug a very attractive parishioner. You can bet Julia shops somewhere else now.

4. Who was a paladin besides Richard Boone?

One of Charlemagne's twelve heroic nights (and eleven fun-filled days). They were to Charlemagne what the Round Table was to the Algonquin.

5. Was Lincoln's mole on his left cheek or his right?

Right. His cheeks were often turned in photos. The rule of thumb is if you see a man in a stovepipe hat with a growth on his left cheek, you're looking at a Lincoln impersonator.

6. Who—by everybody's admission—was "the most perfect" couple in high school?

Danny Peters and Adele Hootkin.

7. Why is water blue?

Vanish. If the water is outdoors, it may be blue because water refracts the blue end of the spectrum. This is also why a newborn's eyes look blue even when they eventually turn out to match her mother's.

8. If you're looking for religion, where in the Dewey decimal system will you find it?

    a. *200s*
    b. *500s*
    c. *700s*

    a. *One Dewey (George) steamed into Manila and was immortalized, and the other (Melvil) steamed into the card catalogs and was lost forever (in the 800s).*

9. "Ma is a nun, as I am," is an example of what?

    a. *a synopsis of a new show on the Fox network*
    b. *why some people should not drink, particularly altar wine*
    c. *a palindrome*

    c. *People obsessed with palindromes generally look the same coming or going.*

10. Illustrate the "first position" in ballet.

    Good, but your toes should be pointed out, and your heels back to back. Plus, lose the street shoes.

11. Who's higher, a duke, an earl, or the Duke of Earl?

    Although "The Duke of Earl" went to number one, a duke is about as high as you can get outside the immediate royal family. It goes something like this: 1. Prince 2. Duke 3. Spot.

12. Where would you find an inverted pyramid?

In a newspaper story, where you start with a foregone conclusion and work backward, after first neglecting to check your sources.

13. The moon is given a month to encircle the earth. How much time does it have left over to slough off?

Eleven hours, fifteen minutes, and fifty-seven point two seconds.

14. Should you be in a completely medieval humor, you would be in "blood," "back bile," "yellow bile," and what?

You would be in phlegm, and longing for the Renaissance.

15. What's a philippic?

Any attack on a guy named Philip (or Phil), but particularly the ones Demosthenes rattled off against Philip II, the King of Macedon. Demosthenes, the original demagogue, referred to the first great modern king and father of Alexander the Great as "a pestilent fellow of Macedon, a country from which we never get even a decent slave." Aristotle was very fond of him, though.

16. Is Earth round?

No, it bulges at the center, as seen in full-length mirrors boosted into orbit.

17. A story problem: A television evangelist owes a half million dollars in fines for defrauding his flock. If he earns eleven cents an hour making wicker hampers, he will have paid his debt to society in how many hours?

Four and a half million. And when he finishes, Tammy Faye won't even be waiting.

• Deep Background:

What Was the Role of Dogs in the Revolutionary War?

On March 5, 1770, the first canines, believed to have been mixed breeds, gave their lives in the American struggle for independence, when two dogs, along with seven colonists, were killed by the British in the Boston Massacre. The scene, immortalized in an etching by eyewitness Paul Revere, shows a dog in the forefront of the American ranks as they faced British rifles. The senseless slaying of the friendly mongrels did as much to raise colonial hackles as any of the Intolerable Acts.

The Deity's position in the War of Independence was arguable, but both armies could claim dog on their side. Francis Marion, the Swamp Fox, smelled out Lord Cornwallis with dogs, and a colonial rival of Washington's, Charles Lee, was said to trust no one but his dogs, a sentiment that many thought should have made it to the coinage. Washington himself was a lover of foxhounds, although his wife was not. The Battle of Harlem Heights in Manhattan was delayed when British General Howe's foxhound, Duchess, was returned to Howe after wandering into Washington's tent. In gratitude, Howe sent Washington a bottle of claret and the battle continued.

---

18. Someone who pays attention to punctilios is punctilious, all right, but what is she really?

She is really looking right over my shoulder. I'd have to say the extreme and incessant scrutiny of details can be a positive attribute, particularly if you're a zeppelin inspector.

19. Construct a simple battery using only things found around the house.

All right, but be prepared to replace the three lemons she was saving for the red snapper. And don't forget to put the fish back in the tank.

20. Mellifluous, literally, means filled with what?

Mellif: *"filled with honey," from the Latin. Generally meaning "sweet sounding," "music to your ears." Don't believe it.*

21. Someone has written *megapod* on your gym locker. What is he/she implying?

That your footprints in the hall caused a Bigfoot scare.

22. Why was it a good idea not to look at the Gorgons?

Just one look and you have a heart (and organs) of stone, and can only work as a gargoyle or a graveyard angel. The ones you want to avoid are the winged sisters, Euryale, Medusa, and Stheno. The other one (Bernice) is really quite nice.

23. Before it was a TV show whose premise I still can't figure out, what was a "quantum leap?"

A sudden alteration in the energy level of an atom or molecule, or a metaphor, much misused, hyperbolizing some superficial change, e.g. "a quantum leap in sandwich freshness." Now, why is the guy in a dress every other week? And why does nobody care?

24. OK, then what's a hyperbole?

An obvious exaggeration for the sake of effect, e.g. "'til death do you part."

25. Who, of the following, was not a French explorer?

    a. *La Salle*
    b. *Chevrolet*
    c. *De Soto*

    b. *On the other hand, the other two are not cars anymore.*

26. Which president, not known for his intellectual prowess, said, "I know somewhere there is a book that will give me the truth, but, hell, I couldn't read the book."

Warren Harding, who is said once to have cried when he couldn't understand a tax proposal. Or maybe he did understand it.

27. You mean to tell me Ohio was part of the Northwest Territory?

Yes, I do. Along with Wisconsin, Indiana, Illinois, Michigan, and part of Minnesota. That would have made Georgia and Arkansas the heart of the Midwest and only the beginning of the confusion, what with Milwaukee in the East and the White Sox in the West.

28. The only things wrong with the Holy Roman Empire, Voltaire said, were what?

It "was neither holy, nor Roman, nor an Empire." (See punctilious, above.) This can be used with only slightly less effect in other situations, e.g., "The only things wrong with the Universal Pricing Code is . . ." or "Minnesota Mining and Manufacturing . . ."—but I wouldn't overdo it.

29. A strong reaction involving subjective feelings of unpleasantness and agitation accompanied by widespread activity of the sympathetic nervous system is known as what?

Fear. For those of you who don't know the meaning of.

30. Explain how—in this day and age—anything can be Post-Modern.

31. After reading *The Prince,* did your means justify your ends, or your ends your means?

I don't know, but they say ballot boxes from the student-council elections are still on the bottom of Lake Michigan.

32. What advice was Bo Peep given on recovering her sheep?

"Leave them alone and they'll come home." It's just this sort of permissiveness that led to the sixties.

33. Let's see, an "idiocrasy"; that'd be rule by idiots, wouldn't it?

No, you're thinking of the two-party system. An "idiocrasy" is the same as an "idiosyncrasy," one of those little things you do that you think makes you so endearing.

34. Why isn't meteorology the study of meteors?

"Meteor" literally means anything up in the air, hence, the application to weather prediction.

35. What's so noble about a noble gas?

A noble gas is too far above other gasses to easily get into relationships with them—an inert gas with exactly zero valence. Helium, neon, argon, krypton, xenon, and radon all have this reputation.

36. What was the IGY that *Our Weekly Reader* kept touting in 1957?

International Geophysical Year, during which a concerted and cooperative study of Earth by scientists of all ilks was supposed to occur. The Russians celebrated by launching Sputnik, really putting a damper on the party. Then they went and abandoned Project Mohole, which now just gathers rain water.

37. Why isn't "priceless" the same as "free"?

Good question. Apparently some things don't have a price on them because they're worth too much, and some because they're worth too little, or maybe somebody removed the tag. You never see a "priceless" pile at a garage sale—at least around here.

38. How do you spell *accommodate?*

There you are. Let me know if there's anything more I can do.

39. Do you need a corpse for a corpus delicti?

No, although it might contribute dramatic effect. Any object upon which a crime has been committed will do. A head, for example, in the case of a bad haircut.

40. Is a nook the same as a cranny?

No, and don't let either ever hear you say it. A nook is a corner, while a cranny is a crevice or a fissure. Despite being continually lumped together (like flora and fauna), they couldn't be more different.

41. Can a man be a debutante?

Yes, but he can't wear the dress, even if he drops the e. Men, generally, don't come out, though, ever.

42. Complete: Nature and Consuela abhor . . .

A vacuum.

43. Give an example of an involuntary response.

44. Did Jefferson or Franklin invent the dumbwaiter?

Jefferson. Also the monetary system and the folding attic ladder. If he ever could have concentrated on one thing, he would have been great.

45. How many mattresses can a princess feel a pea through?

Twenty, at least, and twenty eiderdowns, as well, according to Hans Christian Andersen.

46. The half-life of uranium 238 is four and a half billion years. In nine billion, will all of it be gone?

Oh, if it were only that simple. No, it decays by half every four and a half billion years, so you're just sweeping it under the rug.

47. What the heck is a legume again?

Your beans, your peas, in general your nitrogen-fixing seed-pod plants which add nitrogen to the soil, making the crops on the subsequent shift green without envy.

• Deep Background:

What Were Gunfights Really Like in the Old West?

Gunfights in the Old West were pretty much hit-and-miss affairs, due to the inaccuracy of most sidearms of the day and the amount of bracing required before stepping into the street. One, between Judge William M. Gwin and Joseph McCorkle outside of San Francisco in 1855, was not untypical.

Since the duel was some miles from his home, Gwin thoughtfully arranged for a messenger on horseback to convey the outcome to his wife. That afternoon, the messenger raced to the Gwin house and shouted, "The first fire has been exchanged and no one is hurt!" Mrs. Gwin, needless to say, was greatly relieved, as she was on the second and third occasions that afternoon when given the same news. When the messenger arrived for the fourth time he was invited to dinner, during the course of which he asked Mrs. Gwin's reaction to the fourth volley being fired and no one being hit. "I think," Mrs. Gwin is reported to have replied, "that there has been some mighty poor shooting."

The shoot-out continued late into the night, ending with neither party suffering so much as a graze. Gwin went on to become the first governor of California, by which time we can assume the story to have improved considerably.

———————————————

48. Which former president of the United States was drafted by the Green Bay Packers?

Gerald "Stumbles" Ford. But they had the good sense not to use him.

49. "A foolish consistency is the ——— of little minds."

Hobgoblin, of course, or so said Emerson, but, remember, being inconsistent doesn't make you a genius.

50. What's a Pooh-Bah?

No, it doesn't like honey; it's someone who holds several positions giving him/her ample opportunity to demonstrate incompetence across the board. From The Mikado.

51. Were the Pilgrims Communists?

Yes, according to a microfilm discovered in a pumpkin at the first Thanksgiving. According to Richard Shenkman they were, although communalists *might be more apt. All supplies were pooled at first, but discontent soon arose among those who felt they deserved more and those who felt others deserved less.*

52. Is a "pullet" a boy chicken or a girl chicken?

A girl, less than a year old.

53. What's the difference between a coup d'état and a Coupe de Ville?

The grill?

54. If a peduncle isn't the guy married to your pedaunt, what is it?

The stem of a flower, you little pistil.

55. When you're in flagrante delicto what are you?

Right in the middle of an obvious delicto.

56. As far as rocks go, you've got your sedimentary, your igneous, and your:

Metamorphic, your born-again rocks, like quartz.

57. Besides a kitchen cleanser, who was Ajax?

Not to be confused with the lesser Ajax, the Great Ajax was the hero of the Trojan War who rescued the body of Achilles, who, as you remember, forgot to wear his Hightops. Ajax, perhaps too sensitive for a warrior, killed himself when Achilles' armor was given to Odysseus, who, after all, was no slacker himself.

58. What started in 1618 and ended in 1648?

You'd be surprised how many people say the Hundred Years' War.

59. A real old coot would be what?

An aquatic bird of the genus Fulica *of considerable age.*

60. Is a *howdah* a seat on the back of an elephant or a form of greeting in Muscle Shoals, Alabama?

Both.

61. The starched collar that made a Renaissance man look like his head was a party favor was called what?

A ruff.

62. Would it be fair to call a plane curve formed by the intersection of a right circular cone with a plane parallel to the generator of the cone a parabola?

Yes, it would be more than fair.

63. Had you paid attention in biology, you'd know why your skin is flaking away. Why?

Because it's dead, that's why. Face it, your epidermis is a slag heap of defunct keratin, and no amount of Oil of Olay is going to stick it together again.

64. Fred Allen said, "You can take all the ———— in Hollywood, place it in the navel of a fruit fly and still have room enough for three caraway seeds and a producer's heart."

Sincerity. We could do with a little less Emerson in school and a little more Fred Allen.

65. Not to be confused with a Popsicle (a registered trademark), what is an "ossicle"?

A small bone. If found in Popsicle, see attorney.

66. "Into the room the women come and go, speaking of

  a. *Vincent van Gogh"*
  b. *Michelangelo"*
  c. *the latest in garden hoes."*

b. Although some of the women may have been speaking of "c" "The Weasel."

67. After you're a larva you're a

Pupa. After you're a pupa, though, you could be a moth if you're not careful.

68. What kind of a crowd is a "motley" crowd?

Diverse. Should be a compliment. Isn't.

69. What's the difference between algae and fungi?

Fungi just want to have fun. As the alga said to the fungus, "We're both simple plants. Just because I have chlorophyll and you don't shouldn't make a difference." (But, in the end, an aerobic should never marry an anaerobic.)

70. What was the *S* for in Harry S Truman?

S. Mr. Truman stuck it in there to have something between the Harry *and the* Truman. *To his credit, he didn't use a period after it since—unlike Mr. Truman—it really didn't stand for anything.*

● Deep Background:
_____

Who First Made Money?

While jade, salt, amber, skins, and gold were bartered as early as 3000 B.C., the first universal medium of exchange was probably cattle, the breeding of which produced interest. The nomadic Aryans traded oxen and consequently drove a hard bargain. Indeed, the Latin word for money, *pecunia,* comes from the word *pecus,* or cattle. While cattle were more portable than the heavy iron ingots exchanged by the Macedonians, their disadvantage was that it was nearly impossible to make change without a butcher.

The first coin was the silver shekel of the Babylonians, which became so much the rage of the ancient world that nations lined up to conquer Babylon to get more. In about 2000 B.C., the Servants of the Temple of the Moon God of Ur, the original traveling salesmen, took a giant step for mankind by never leaving home without letters of credit on clay tablets advising creditors to see the Moon God for payment. The Carthaginians, considered the first modern traders, developed "leather money," a promise on parchment to pay the bearer on demand the stipulated amount of gold. Unfortunately, the bearers all showed up at once and Carthage was sacked.

Small change was an innovation of the Athenians, who minted exceedingly small silver coins, some nearly the size of a pinhead which (due to pocketless togas) were carried in the mouth. Often as not, when money circulated in Athens, it really circulated.

---

71. Something sticking in your craw would be sticking where again?

Your stomach. Quite a bit sticks in my craw these days.

72. Given a circle with *A* as its center and as many points as you want on the circumference, describe a sector.

A piece of cake. Easy as ABC.

73. Why don't the Yaps have vending machines?

The coins are twelve feet across in Micronesia.

74. Are Warsaw and Athens very nearly on the same latitude or the same longitude?

Longitude—approximately twenty degrees east. But if you follow Milwaukee straight down, you'll pretty much run into the Galapagos Islands. If Darwin had studied Milwaukee, the course of evolution would have been considerably altered, or abandoned altogether.

75. What body of water has Africa on one side, Europe on the other, and the Middle East just around the corner?

The very handy Mediterranean Sea.

76. When your malleus pounds on your incus, you're

    a. *in love*
    b. *running on your rims*
    c. *hearing*

c. This is not to neglect the tympanic membrane or the stapes, all part of the equation, or the Miracle-Ear, for that matter.

77. Does a Holstein produce large quantities of milk low in butterfat, or small quantities of milk high in butterfat?

The former, which is why they are evolutionarily desirable, and damn affectionate, besides.

78. What did Sandburg mean when he said, "Poetry is the achievement of the synthesis of hyacinths and biscuits"?

I don't know—as a garnish, maybe?

79. Scottish economist Adam Smith is associated with what philosophy of the marketplace?

"The Theory of Moral Sentiments," in which markets are left to their own devices and an "invisible hand" picks the pockets of the populace.

80. How are you classified zoologically?

A vertebrate, most of the time. Overall (remember) it goes (in descending order): phyla/classes/orders/families/species/ radio hosts.

81. I have a cylinder I want to fill with a fluid of my choice. How do I figure out how much I need?

Easy: $V = r^2 \times pi \times height$. What do you mean, fluid of your choice?

82. What do Levi P. Morton, Garret A. Hobart, and Alben W. Barkley all have in common?

They all have names you don't hear much anymore, probably because they were vice presidents of the United States, under Harrison, McKinley, and Truman, respectively. J. Danforth Quayle, J. Danforth Quayle, . . .

83. Did Wyatt Earp die of natural causes?

Yup. With his boots off, in Los Angeles in 1929 at age eighty-one.

84. The *Rx* in prescriptions: What does it mean?

Take! from the Latin recipe. This to appease Jupiter, the Roman god of pharmacy, whose considerable orbs used to hang in the window. A better question would be, Why do pharmacists stand on elevated platforms?

85. In the event of a plague upon your White House, who's most likely to succeed first: the Secretary of Health and Human Services or the Secretary of Housing and Urban Development?

Health—which leads me to believe the plague was no accident. Both are scraping the bottom of the Cabinet, though.

86. Who is known as "the father of canning"?

a. *Benjamin Franklin*
b. *Napoleon*
c. *Marquis de Sade*

b. *Not content to be the father of the Paris sewer system, Napoleon, in 1809, offered a prize of twelve thousand francs (in those days worth twelve thousand francs) for the best way to preserve food for his troops, who were planning a little tour. Nicolas-François Appert—himself the father of bouillon cubes—came up with glass jars. Thus Napoleon's observation, "An army travels on its Ball jars."*
The Marquis was the father of caning.

87. I am gable and I am hip. I am a lean-to. I am gambrel and mansard. What am I?

A roof.

88. If your Italian teacher calls you *punchinello*, what is he implying?

That you lack a certain decorum, perhaps? That you are, in fact, absurd, ridiculous, or grotesque?

89. If you need *E. coli bacteria*, where's a surefire place to look for them?

A salad bar or the human intestine. These little devils are not only a boon to digestion, they are highly prized for recombinant DNA work.

90. Who wrote

> Sure, deck your lower limbs in pants;
> Yours are the limbs, my sweeting.
> You look divine as you advance—
> Have you seen yourself retreating?

Ogden Nash, who obviously wore the pants in his family.

91. What's an ovipositor?

Any device for depositing eggs, particularly in an insect.

92. Plato said which internal organ is "a mirror in which the thoughts of the mind fall reflected as the image of the soul"?

The liver, still very popular in France. The Greeks of old believed the liver to be the center of strength and courage, which is why, when a vulture gnawed it away, it added insult to injury.

93. What was Cassandra's problem?

Cassandra (modern: Consuela) was a prophetess no one believed, all because she rebuffed Apollo who, having given her the forecasting gift, attached a small disclaimer. Sometimes you wonder how some guys got to be gods.

94. What ever became of Pangaea?

You're thinking of the original land mass, some 230 million years ago (boy, how time flies!) which, during the Paleo-

zoic, lost its moorings and began to drift, finally being torn asunder into a southern Gondwanaland and a northern Laurasia.

95. Did Alexander the Great wear a beard?

No, he was peachy-faced all his days, a radical departure from world conquerors of the time.

96. What do Iran and Nebraska have in common?

A unicameral legislature (Nebraska's is the only one in the United States).

97. The Delphic oracle was known for giving what kind of answers?

    a. *ambiguous*
    b. *couched in heavy parable*
    c. *pointless and error-filled personal reminiscences of his youthful acting days*

    a. *Ambiguous.*

98. When something is so highly ornamental it makes you want to puke, what is it called?

Rococo. If you liked foliage around your furniture, you were in heaven.

99. Spell "penitentury."

Penitentiary. According to Gallup, one of the hardest words for Americans to spell.

100.   Why are poached eggs against the law in the Ozarks?

Because they come from paddlefish. You can get up to two years in the penta . . . pennatent . . . uh, slammer. This is a trick question, and was put in just to lower the curve.

101.   What's the difference between a national anthem and a national anathema?

No difference, if it's sung by Roseanne Arnold.

102.   Who was the big brother—Orville or Wilbur Wright?

Wilbur. It was Orville's bike he took apart to make the first airplane.

103.   There was a Copper Age and a Bronze Age. Was there a Brass Age?

No—who wants to polish for an Age. Mythologically speaking, the Ages of Man go Golden, Silver, Bronze, and Iron, which, here in the rust belt, anyway, we're still in. Historically, one may speak of the Stone, Bronze, Iron, and the current Particle Board.

104.   In poetry, is *hexameter* a dactylic line of six feet in which the first four feet are dactyls or spondees, the fifth is ordinarily a dactyl, and the last is a trochee or spondee with a caesura usually following the long syllable in the third foot?

Yes.

105. The New World might still not be discovered were it not for the unquenchable passion for what?

a. *landfill*
b. *a site for the new prison*
c. *pepper*

c. *In those days, a man was judged by the size of his pepper mill, which, being a man, he carried with him at all times. Columbus's pitch to Isabella was that he could deliver the pepper. People kept their pepper in a sock under the mattress because they didn't believe in banks. I saw a whole hour of this on PBS and can tell you more if you'd like to know.*

106. If you kow-tow to the assistant vice-principal, what are you doing?

Probably a wash and possibly a wax. Still, it beats serving twelve detentions. Literally, to knock one's head on the floor or ground in front of an authority, making an impression on both.

107. Trivia is, in fact:

No small thing, but the Roman goddess of the crossroads, sorcery, and hounds. That's a lot of responsibility.

108. Where can you drive with poetic license?

Anywhere they don't hold conventions.

109. If you're eccentric, what are you?

One of two circles not having the same center one within the other, or English.

110. If you're told that your fallacy is pathetic, what have you probably slipped into doing again?

Assigning human attributes to nature, or to someone in your family. (Like "Ol' Man River," which does both.)

111. A relationship in which two organisms live together for mutual benefit is called

Symbiosis. This occurs in all nature outside of human. Symbiotic relationships were all the rage in the seventies, particularly between flowering plants and a wide range of insects.

112. Kangaroo babies are called

Joeys. You can call your baby Joey, too, if you want.

113. The Greek suffix *-gamy* means literally what?

Marriage. So electrogamy would mean marriage between wiring; telegamy, being married to the phone; photogamy would mean wedding pictures; and matrigamy would be the result of falling in love with love.

114. What's wrong with this next sentence? Every one of the mechanics knew they had to bring their own wrenches.

Besides the obvious fact that some mechanics will claim they were never told to bring wrenches, you should probably substitute he *and* his *wrenches, particularly if they're Snap-On, as he will never be happy with (even) Sears's best.*

115. What do calories—say the five hundred in a Quarter Pounder with cheese—actually measure?

How much heat you'd produce if you could get it to burst into flame. There have been documented cases of quarter pounders bursting into flame for no apparent reason, leaving behind just a pair of slippers and an open copy of one of the "Rabbi" mysteries.

116. What kind of swoop is a "fell swoop"?

A fierce one, not unlike a bird of prey, although, unless you started from a thousand feet, not like one.

117. Is Mars actually red, or are those just your eyes, Dad?

It's actually red, not some silly distortion in Earth's atmosphere (like so many things nowadays). The soil is sort of red clay, like Georgia, but, unlike Georgia, Mars never gets above twenty below, and the atmosphere is so thin your blood boils whether you're mad or not.

118. Who—or what—does "paradiddles"?

What. A drummer.

119. If you're accused of being "amorphous," what is it you are rumored not to have?

A shape. This is the trouble with arguing with some smarty-pants: You never know what they're calling you.

• ___Deep Background___:

What Was the War of Griffin's Pig?

The War of Griffin's Pig, one of the longest conflicts in American history, stemmed from a jurisdictional dispute between British Columbia and the United States over San Juan Island near Vancouver, settled and claimed by both Britain and the United States.

On June 15, 1859, Lamar A. Cutler, an American, discovered the black boar of Charles Griffin, a British national, rooting in his potato patch. Acting under what he later called "the impulse of the moment," Cutler shot the hog. Griffin called the act "wanton murder," and appealed to British authorities, who dispatched the warship *Satellite* to arrest Cutler.

Cutler sought the protection of Brigadier General W. S. Haney, the American Army commander, who obligingly landed on the island nine infantry companies supported by artillery. The British responded with over two thousand infantrymen, including the Royal Marines, and anchored five dreadnaughts offshore. Haney was pondering his next move when relieved of command by President Buchanan, who thought things were getting a little out of ham (*sic*).

The dispute was not actually settled until 1872, when an arbitrator, peace-loving Kaiser Wilhelm I of Germany, awarded San Juan Island to the United States, and a black boar to Charles Griffin.

---

120. Where might you find a *ubiquitous* person?

> *Where wouldn't you? This was a word people used before the much more lyrical "in your face."* Omnipresent; *although, you never hear God referred to as ubiquitous (nor do the righteous proclaim "God is in my face").*

121. The girdle around Earth's swelling midsection between the Tropics of Cancer and Capricorn is referred to as the

> *Torrid Zone. Probably doesn't mean much; we're supposed to be in the Temperate.*

122. What does *e pluribus unum* mean?

> *From many messes, one big one.*

123.   Is being called the penultimate almost as good as being called the ultimate?

Not unless you like being next to last.

124.   Without using your hands, describe the shape of an Erlenmeyer flask.

Right, that's why it's used for swishing.

125.   Quick, which elephant has the little ears?

The Indian. Well, all right; three feet across is not little.

126.   The tendency for the liquids in your tubes to rise is explained by what phenomenon?

Capillary action. Do you realize that life could not exist if fluids didn't rise in tubes? That the nose on your face is the result of petrochemical technology? That the odor that they put in gas smells exactly like your house does ordinarily?

127.   Jason and the Argonauts set out in quest of what trophy with magical powers?

The Golden Fleece. Still, it didn't work for the golden ram. The Golden Fleece was said to have originally covered the car seats of Aetes, king of Colchis. I seem to remember a daughter, as well, and that Jason looked like Victor Mature.

128. The five "W's" are:

> *Who? What? Where? When? Why? In school, this is what you ask when told that someone unlikelier than you scored over the weekend.*

129. You have four options: wind, water, ejection, or animals. What are you?

> *A seed awaiting dispersal. And, frankly, you can wait your whole life and never get dispersed, or get dispersed, but in the totally wrong place. So, despite the options, there are no guarantees.*

Science

● **WHEN WE WERE KIDS,** my friend Teddy and I were
going to be bachelor scientists and share a duplex. This
may sound a little strange to you, but you should know every
Milwaukee dream ends ". . . and share a duplex." Our greatest
discovery was gunpowder, which (I realize) the Chinese claim,
but we discovered could be assembled with nonprescription
ingredients from the drugstore on Sixtieth Street. If they asked
about the saltpeter, you were just to say it was for your
brother's lunches. We had an explosive device that could blow
open a milk-chute door, helping make them obsolete. Fortunately, puberty intervened before we got to car bombs;
unfortunately, sharing a duplex was no longer a consideration.

My brother Arthur had a science lab in the basement,

formerly Howard's Sports Central, and, when he'd let me, I'd watch him euthanize butterflies and make horrible smells in a test tube (one of Dad's cigar tubes, really) over his Bunsen burner. Arthur and I together captured the legendary "bird shit" butterfly (actually a moth, but that didn't sound as good), a miracle of adaptation that exactly mimicked a bird dropping on the fender of one of the used cars in the Uptown Motors lot. In all the years since, I've never seen another bird shit butterfly fly away, and believe me, I've waited. Arthur snared that one, mounted it on a pin under a cigar tube, and Mother threw it away, setting entomology back a generation of brothers (or, possibly forever, as the bird shit's natural habitat, Uptown Motors, is no longer there).

Although that chloroformed the naturalist in me, I never lost my interest in science, although I soon discovered I was not built for the scientific method. I would much rather jump to conclusions and work backward. Years later, I discovered that's what scientists *do,* and some of them make pretty good money at it, too. But by then it was too late; I was hell-bent on the humanities track after a near disaster in general science when, finding myself on a lab stool next to leggy Chris Crum, I poured sulfuric acid in my lap.

It was impossible, of course, but I would have loved to have shared a duplex with her; we could have been the Pasteurs.

1. How long were there fishes before there were fishhooks?

    a. *a billion years*
    b. *500 million years*
    c. *250 million years*

    b. *They never saw a guy with a creel until a mere fourteen thousand years ago. Now they look at them all day.*

2. If the sun were blown out (say on God's birthday), how long before we would know the party's over?

    a. *two minutes*
    b. *four minutes*
    c. *eight minutes*

    c. *Just as well—what do you get a deity who has everything?*

3. According to research conducted at Washington University, blinking not only moistens the eyes, it

    a. *soothes the savage breast*
    b. *indicates thinking is occurring*
    c. *reveals heightened sexual interest*

    b. *This is an extremely important finding for people who want people to think they're thinking. Unfortunately, if these people aren't blinking, they're not thinking about anything. An indicator of heightened sexual interest (although not the best) is dilated pupils. Blinking eyes with dilated pupils results in goo-goo eyes.*

4. Can a rabbit and a hare mate?

No. And marriage is out of the question.

5. In a study in London, women overestimated the size of their chests, waists, and hips. Which did they overestimate the most?

Waists—by 28 percent, although they thought their chests were 24 percent bigger and their hips 16 percent. Many are fine slips of girls, and don't realize it.

6. True or false? Smart people's brains use less energy.

True. A study at the University of California-Irvine found that high-IQ brains consume less blood sugar and they run cooler, possibly because many have crew cuts and are air-cooled.

7. According to a USDA study, what percentage of boars have sexual problems?

One in five—some thirty-five thousand in this country alone. Some male boars are simply not unattractive enough to be appealing to females.

8. Did Neolithic man cultivate grain for bread or beer?

Beer, according to Dr. S. H. Katz at the University of Pennsylvania, or that's what he would have done, anyway. Makes sense. Beer is one big step for mankind up from gruel, keeps well, and takes your mind off how much you still have to evolve.

9. True or false? Sea cows can be aggressive when aroused.

> *False. According to narrator William Forsythe (Sirens of the Sea, A&E cable), who, after all, was a bachelor father, they're completely lacking in aggression. It may be a moot point, however, since they are indiscriminate during mating and have been known to love a log to splinters. The best thing to come out of this show was the notion that sea cows, mistaken for mermaids, lured sailors to their deaths on rocky reefs. I know a man gets lonely at sea, but that lonely?*

10. Are the potoos of Central America related to the goatsuckers of Europe?

> *Yes. They are both nocturnal birds of a feather. The goatsucker, by the way, does not suck goats, but insects scooped up in flight. It is almost impossible to scoop up goats in flight. False but persistent charges of vampirism account for the goatsuckers' unfortunate moniker.*

11. "Bradykinin" is a chemical secretion of the body produced at the site of an injury. What critical function does it perform?

> *It produces pain. Without it, we wouldn't know we were in pain and life would lose its meaning. Without pain, of course, pleasure would have no meaning, although we could probably come up with one easy enough. When pain occurs, brandykinin is the best treatment.*

12. What's happening with oysters in months without an *r* in them?

a. *not much—you?*
b. *they're reproducing*
c. *they're on shore leave*

b. *Ironically, their meat becomes soft when they reproduce.*

13. Why are researchers at Cornell fitting chickens with prescription lenses with the wrong correction?

To see which street they cross. All right, they claim to be studying eye adaptation to see if bad eyes can be corrected into good ones. Personally, I think they're just a bunch of jokers over there.

14. Do college undergraduates find two-faced or thirty-two-faced people more attractive?

Thirty-two-faced. The more faces that went into a composite drawing, the more attractive it was deemed to be. And yet, try to get them to look at a Picasso.

15. One of the wonders of the Amazon rain forest, the hoatzin, or cowbird, resembles a cow in what way?

a. *its udderlike comb*
b. *its manurelike ambience*
c. *its tendency to stand facing the same direction as the rest of the flock*

b. *The cowbird is one big flying crop, which is why all vehicles in the Amazon should be garaged.*

16. A trout in May will eat only

    a. *size-eight mayflies*
    b. *size-ten mayflies*
    c. *size-fourteen mayflies*

    c. *According to the* San Francisco Chronicle, *trout are "not Rhodes scholars," but they're unbeatable at sizing mayflies. Mayflies, my trout source, Lynn Blenker, tells me, get smaller as their number gets larger, so you'd have to eat two fourteens if you were hungry for a seven.*

17. What kind of cloud is the Oort cloud?

    A huge swarm of comets, at a distance from us of between one thousand and one hundred thousand times the distance to the sun. From here they look like a swarm of number fourteens.

18. How many bee miles are flown to make one pound of honey?

    None of your beeswax. Oh, all right, 640,000: 40,000 bee loads, or some 80,000 beelines.

19. If you're a fox and you want to eat a hedgehog that has rolled up into a spiny ball, what's the recommended procedure?

    Take a medium-size hedgehog and roll the little critter into a pool of water; when the hedgehog uncurls to swim, eat.

• Deep Background:

Can Aging Be Reversed?

Well, you could try losing a few, squeezing what's left into a pair of button flies, and making the scene at Shooters on Friday night, but odds are you'd end up feeling even older. More promising is the work being done by Dr. Daniel Rudman, a gerontologist at the Medical College of Wisconsin in Milwaukee, who has turned back the biological clocks of test subjects twenty years by giving them human growth hormone. His subjects, twenty-eight men between the ages of sixty and eighty, became, within a matter of months, twenty-eight men between the ages of forty and sixty. Dr. Rudman believes that one of the primary causes of aging is a deficiency in growth hormone beginning in middle age, leading to this (here) in men, and that (there) in women, and, eventually, to the frailties often associated with advanced years. The men in Rudman's study not only saw the degeneration of their muscle, bone, and endocrine systems stop, many went out looking for dime-a-dance girls.

Taking another approach, Walter Pierpaoli of the Institute for Medical Research in Switzerland, has been experimenting with the hormone melatonin, a secretion of the pineal gland, in an attempt to reset the body's biological clock and fool it into thinking it's eleven A.M. instead of P.M. Pierpaoli fed melatonin-laced water to laboratory rats and his eighty-two-year-old mother-in-law, who, as a result, now feels good enough to actively interfere in his marriage again, demonstrating that these therapies, while promising, are not without their costs.

---

20. Whose brain was bigger: Neanderthal man's or your neighbor Ed Schmitz's?

> *Despite the superficial resemblance, Neanderthal's. Not only has Neanderthal man been much maligned for his cranial capacity, he always returned ladders.*

21. Do female guppies prefer intellectual or brightly colored males?

> *You have to ask? They like the flashy orange ones, naturally, and so do predators.*

22. How many calories do you burn sleeping?

> *Between 60 and 70 per hour, more if you saw wood. This is about the same as watching television, and exactly the same if TV has the same effect on you as it has on me. Being sedentary, by the way, burns up to 150 calories per hour, so you may want to work up to it.*

23. If you never forget a face, you can thank your ———— hemisphere.

> *Right. If you never remember a name, however, you can blame your—whatchacallit?—your left.*

24. Is spaghetti good for depression?

Yes. Carbohydrates produce the amino acid tryptophan, which tends to make women sleepy and men calmer. The spaghetti has to be taken every two hours, however.

25. College students, asked to press a lever every time they have a sexual thought, would press it

   a. *one hundred*
   b. *two hundred*
   c. *three hundred times a day*

   c. *"Over," according to Dr. Harold Lief, University of Pennsylvania pioneer of desire. The only known antidote is graduate school.*

26. What percentage of human genetic material is filler?

Ninety-five percent. Only 5 percent—between fifty thousand and one hundred thousand genes—are needed to build a human; the rest are there because of the various trade unions.

27. If you slithered like a snake instead of walking the way you do, would you conserve energy?

No, and you'd look damn silly besides. Both lateral undulation and concertina locomotion use more energy than putting one foot in front of the other—so knock it off.

28. What percentage of baby birds are born out of wedlock?

Thirty percent. This is the real story of the birds and the bees.

29. Venus has continents with the consistency of

a. *peanut butter*
b. *cheese curds*
c. *melba toast*

a. *Venus has two continents that will stick to the roof of your mouth, Ishtar Terra (not the one with Warren Beatty) and Aphrodite Terra (you might look for Warren here).*

30. Mouse-tailed, hare-lipped, hollow-faced, horseshoe-nosed, big-eared, hammer-headed, and tube-nosed are all varieties of what mammal?

Bats, order Chiroptera. *And they wonder why they get a bad press.*

31. How do galaxies with tails get them?

a. *they're born with them*
b. *after big bangs into other galaxies*
c. *they're extruded by the vacuumlike suction of nearby black holes*

b. *Cosmologists with tails, however, are born with them.*

32. Do eunuchs have a higher or lower rate of heart disease than the festooned male?

Lower, although that's small comfort.

33. According to Malcomb Brown in *The New York Times,* do "certain sperm cells seem to play an altruistic role"?

> *Yes, but it may be just a line. Some act as blockers in an offensive line for their favored halfback sperm, while others have been known to throw themselves on a spermicide.*

34. According to the *Guinness Book of World Records,* Hideaki Tamoyori of Japan can remember how many digits of pi?

> *Forty thousand. After that, he's totally at sea.*

35. According to the Society for Investigative Dermatology, are bald men more virile?

> *Yes—than dead men. Otherwise, there appears to be no way to substantiate the oft-made claim (of bald men), at least none I'd care to witness. Baldness demonstrates an increased ability to use testosterone, not to produce it.*

36. You have undoubtedly noticed the tendency of the universe toward entropy, haven't you?

> *Yes, yes, the uniformity, the sameness, day in, day out, that can only come from living in one universe too long.*

37. According to the Athena Institute for Women's Wellness, if you take sweat from assorted underarms of various women and rub it on the upper lips of others three times a week, what happens?

> *Party time!*

38. Do nearsighted people appear more intelligent, or are they more intelligent?

Yes. Among subjects with the highest IQs, there is three times the likelihood of nearsightedness, although it might be from all that reading, after all. Myopia and intelligence genes are DNA neighbors, which might account for knocking on the wrong door.

39. According to *Runner's World,* 66 percent of runners think about sex while running. What percentage think about running during sex?

a. *8 percent*
b. *33 percent*
c. *66 percent*

a. *This is why I won't run with just anyone. This and the loud conversations they have running through your neighborhood are two more strikes against this filthy practice.*

40. The greatest danger posed to genetic engineering of plants comes from:

a. *spontaneous mutations due to pollutants*
b. *uprooting by antigenetic alarmists*
c. *random sex with weeds*

c. *Same old story. Even more of a threat than Jeremy Rifkin.*

41. Based on dietary expectations, would man's ancient ancestor *Australopithecus* be able to survive at a Wendy's salad bar?

> *Yes, except for concussions suffered on the sneeze shield. According to the journal* Nature, *he was a salad lover, particularly the garbanzos. Today's vegetarian would find* Australopithecus *a pleasant dinner companion in any smokeless environment.*

• Deep Background:

What Are the Odds That an Asteroid Will Destroy the Earth?

According to NASA scientists, a killer asteroid is pretty much a sure thing unless we do something, and quick, and they're not just saying that because NASA has suffered so many setbacks and funding cuts that the billions needed to produce and man the tracking telescopes and asteroid-diverting rockets would provide them with the major boondoggle that Mars and the space station once promised. Not at all. The Apollo asteroid belt alone strews over a hundred massive extraterrestrial hunks right in our way, and, according to NASA's David Morrison, 99 percent (that's 99 percent!)

of the potential lethal rocks half a kilometer and larger have still not been mapped; they could be anywhere.

In March 1989, an asteroid a half mile across came within four hundred thousand miles of Earth; had it been four hundred thousand miles across, it would have come within a half mile of Earth. Indeed, in 1908 an asteroid struck Siberia with the equivalent force of a ten-megaton nuclear bomb, an event smaller in scale but not unlike that believed to have struck Bermuda (fortunately, during the off season), causing the mass extinction of the dinosaurs. NASA's call to arms, coming as it does just as the likelihood of global nuclear war seems reduced, goes to show you, if it's not one thing it's another.

---

42. What has bug eyes, bristles on its tail, and hasn't seen the light of day for three hundred ninety million years?

> *I don't know, but if it were on your shoulder, you should feel honored. It's the world's oldest insect, a silverfish, discovered in Canada. Apparently they had a food source before your old textbooks in the attic.*

43. Women, despite having more adipose (and—if I may say—more attractively utilized) than men, generally claim to feel colder. Why?

> *Men have higher metabolisms. Particularly around women.*

44. Can light slow down an atom?

Yes, if moving in the opposite direction from the atom, light can push it around. That's why—when you turn on the kitchen light in the middle of the night—the utensils stop dancing.

45. The universe is which?

a. *flat*
b. *curved*
c. *washboardy*

a. *It's like a big Illinois.*

46. We're all of us asymmetrical, but the males of us tend to lean to the

a. *left*
b. *right*
c. *right here and left there*

b. *We grow toward the right, because that's where the light most often is. Women, facing the opposite way, would naturally grow to the left.*

47. Dung beetles can carry off a cow flop in

a. *three hours*
b. *two hours*
c. *one hour*

c. *Or about as long as it takes to read* The *(daily)* New York Times *where this article appeared ("The Dung Dy-*

nasty"). The ancient Egyptians, so advanced in other ways, believed a dung beetle rolled the sun through the heavens.

48. If you started melting the Martian polar caps on Tuesday, how long would it take for the gasses released to make the planet habitable?

    a. *ten thousand years*
    b. *one hundred thousand years*
    c. *should have it for you Thursday, by four o'clock*

    b. *You could do it with mirrors, or cover them with soot, or you could just let NASA try to preserve them.*

49. Who's more likely to associate sex with headaches—men or women?

    Men. "Benign sex headaches," Dr. Seymour Diamond of the Diamond Headache Clinic in Chicago says, "are more common in men, because men tend to exert themselves more during sex." Tend to? We have to.

50. The N-methyl-D-aspartate receptor has just been discovered in your brain. What's it doing there?

    a. *conjuring up Louise, the study-hall monitor in ninth grade*
    b. *making you crave a genuine deli half-done pickle*
    c. *you know it makes you want to shout*

    a. *NMDA is the memory receptor, which could also induce you to think of dill pickles, but between even a good half-done and Louise there was really no choice at all.*

51. According to Dan Powell, the director of the American Institute for Preventive Medicine, which of the following should be loosened?

    a. *shoes*
    b. *shorts*
    c. *ties*

    c. *Dr. Powell advises going tieless, not only because your patients can otherwise grab them, but because they can interrupt the flow of blood to the brain and cause Medicare misbillings.*

52. Do eggs stay fresher stored big or small end down?

    Small. This keeps the yolk nearer the center where it can take the waters of the healthful antibacterial albumen.

53. If you live to be a hundred years old, how many comets might you see?

    a. *a hundred*
    b. *two or three*
    c. *thirty-one*

    a. *There's about one a year visible to the naked eye, although if you started looking in 1911 (a bumper year), you would've chalked up four, and could take three years off.*

54. How long does it take for people to start hating one another in space?

    a. *three to four weeks*
    b. *two to three months*
    c. *eight to nine months*

    c. *This from presidential science adviser Allan Bromley. It would take about eighteen months to reach Mars, by which time astronauts would already be seeing red. Married couples should consider separate capsules. I'm not sure how they came up with this, since some people you'd hate right on the launch pad.*

55. Ninety percent of the variations in Earth's speed are caused by what?

    a. *people shifting their weight*
    b. *wind*
    c. *methane gas emitted by cows*

    b. *The other 10 percent is a wobble from the alignment. Need to take it in.*

56. My alma mater, the University of Wisconsin, is leading the nation in the first known scientific study of rhinotillexomania. What is it?

    Nose picking. A huge rearview mirror will be set up to study drivers at major intersections. Dr. James Jefferson is the man to see for details; that's him over there, up to his knuckle.

57. According to medical researchers in France, are you better off drinking several glasses of red or white wine daily?

Red. But they find it only works with French wine! And, in the best tradition of French medical science, they say the foie gras *is good for you, too. The tannins in a nice Bordeaux are supposed to advance the cause of "good cholesterol," which is the cholesterol Frenchmen have.*

• Deep Background:

What Do They Mean by the Sides of the Brain?

Think of your brain as a walnut (or a cauliflower if you prefer; it's bigger) divided into two hemispheres, each controlling specific functions. The left side, identified with the *I* so often found at the beginning of sentences, is the half that controls speech, adds, subtracts, takes into account, sizes up, makes allowances, rationalizes, tells long pointless stories the right side has heard before, pigeonholes, draws the bottom line, prioritizes, computes interest, seizes the day, names names, makes excuses, and jumps to conclusions. It is the side that came up with this theory. On the other lobe, the right side of the brain is the seat of emotion, music, sex, sensation, the lambada, inspiration, dalliance, visual perceptions, larks, identification of shapes and surfaces, intuition, supposition, insight (real and imagined), great leaps of faith, and uncharacteristic spontaneous behavior that the left side is hard pressed to explain.

It is quite possible that the left side of the brain might not know what the right is doing and vice versa. In experiments with patients whose brains have been surgically split (yes, but they got five dollars an hour for it), it has been proven that a decent game of two-handed canasta is possible with no one else in the room.

---

58. What percentage of success do pike have when stalking their prey?

    a. *50 percent*
    b. *75 percent*
    c. *85 percent*

    b. *A deer hunter with this success rate could be in the tavern by noon on the first day and stay there.*

59. Whose brains get smaller as they age—men's or women's?

Just another nail in the corpus callosum—of men. This is the little doohickey that connects the two halves of the brain. Men's shrink by 20 percent, while you know whose stay the same, or possibly get bigger.

60. Two geologists at Indiana University studying coprolites—fossilized dinosaur dung—believe that dinosaurs contributed to an ancient greenhouse effect. . . . How?

Through flatulence, producing enough methane to warm
up the atmosphere and change the ambience, too. Well,
that's how dinosaur kids knew dad was home.

61. How long until a female rhino who has just given birth
is interested in sex again?

    a. *1 year*
    b. *5 years*
    c. *Sex, shmex*

    b. *You can see how giving birth to a rhino might put you*
off your feed. By five, the little rhino is all big, and it's
time to think about another PBS special.

62. How many lasers can now dance on a pinhead?

    a. *two thousand*
    b. *four thousand*
    c. *ten thousand*

    b. *And still every angel doesn't get one.*

63. Where is the YOU ARE HERE sign in the Milky Way
galaxy?

    a. *three fifths of the way from the center*
    b. *two fifths of the way from the center*
    c. *one fifth of the way from the center*

    a. *We're in the burbs in the Milky Way, although they're*
still building to the west of us.

64. An oceanographer studying currents in the North Pacific used which of the following in his research?

    a. *bands of mackerel on their honeymoon voyage*
    b. *thousands of floating tennis shoes*
    c. *hundreds of gin bottles with hundreds of messages*

    b. *Eighty thousand pairs of Nikes from a South Korean wreck were traced all the way to the Pacific northwestern coastline, where they were gathered and eventually sold off the backs of trucks at the Three Mile Fair in Racine, Wisconsin. Truly, an amazing journey.*

65. The *Magellan* spacecraft has found startling evidence of

    a. *an Elvis Easter Island head on Mars*
    b. *changes in Venus's makeup*
    c. *Freddy Mercury*

    b. *Images taken months apart in 1991 reveal changes in the surface makeup of Venus possibly caused by shifting sand dunes. The Elvis head was discovered by the* National Enquirer.

66. Do termites ever get indigestion?

    No, according to Yang Siqi, director of the Yingtan Termite Research Institute in Beijing. Yang began a lifelong interest in the insects when, after observing the termites' excellent health, he began eating them out of house and home. Not only did his gastritis symptoms disappear, he now has a solid foundation.

67. Could a guy test eggs with the same equipment they use to check nuclear warheads?

    He could, and, in fact, Dipen Sinha of Los Alamos has. Using the same two-dollar Radio Shack speaker (govern-

ment cost: two hundred fifty dollars) he uses to tell what's inside a warhead casing, he has determined that a fresh egg resonates near high G. One small sword beaten into one tiny plowshare.

68. How do cells communicate with one another?

Although it is not known whether cells can hold mirrors outside their membranes to see what's happening in the hallway, they do appear to be able to talk to one another through the air ducts. Small molecules pass from one cell to another through tiny channels called gap junctions, about two billionths of a meter in width. This is how all the cells know if there's going to be a break.

69. Do badgers have love handles?

They do if they're Wisconsin Badgers. But, seriously, nutritionists at the University of California-Davis have discovered that even the leanest of mammals have the same problem areas of fatty deposits as you or I have. It is not uncommon, for example, to find a mother raccoon with a tuchis so monumental her cubs can't squeeze past her in the woods, or a grizzly with a massive bear belly.

70. When's the last time Alaska was balmy?

Well, they say it hit ninety in Anchorage last August, but before that, it was probably a hundred million years ago. The richest fossil flora ever discovered have been found in Alaska, having flourished under a twenty-four-hour sun and sustaining noncrested duckbill hadrosaurs, horned dinosaurs, and Dr. Judith Parrish of the University of Arizona.

71. Can mothers identify their newborns by touch?

Yes. In a study at Hebrew University in Jerusalem, 70 percent of mothers could identify their newborns simply by touching the backs of their cute little hands. Within hours, 100 percent could pick their little behinds out of a lineup.

72. It's four o'clock on Friday; your boss needs ten billion copies of a DNA chain. Can you do it and still catch the five-seventeen?

No problem. A polymerase chain reaction (PCR) can produce billions of copies of the DNA proteins in an hour. But remember, if you leave the flask running over the weekend, you won't be able to find the building for the gene strands.

73. What's a free radical?

Forget William Kunstler; these radicals have been freed by virtue of cell oxidation, during which some molecules are torn apart and thrown out of electrical whack. Free radicals turn butter rancid, and are thought by some scientists to do the same in humans as an important component of aging. Try leaving the butter out and keeping your humans in the refrigerator door.

74. Can a Swiss scientist do a better job at photosynthesis than a coleus?

Yes. The Grätzel-O'Regan photovoltaic cell (Grätzel's the Swiss) is claimed to be "better than the product of a billion years of evolution" in producing electricity from sunlight.

But will talking to your Grätzel-O'Regan produce more voltage?

75. Will a two-headed snake fight over a mouse?

The two-headed black rat snake "IM" at the University of Tennessee will, and for hours. According to Gordon Burghardt, "they're simply fighting for the privilege" of swallowing it, since it ends up in their common stomach. It's tough not to see a metaphor in this, but let's resist.

76. If you'd like to lower your risk of heart attack, should you be shorter or taller?

Hunker up. According to the Harvard Medical School, men five foot seven or shorter had a 60 percent greater risk of a first heart attack than men six foot one or taller.

77. Mass hysteria occurs in how many schools out of a thousand during the school year?

One, although that seems low to me. Typically, during a Trojans' pep rally, or on a Thursday (Sloppy Joes with tater tots). A record sixteen sopranos fainted during a choir concert in Santa Monica in 1989, totally throwing off the harmonies of "My Favorite Things."

78. Do "smart" drugs work?

While most people take drugs to get stupid, which does work, there is no apparent value in taking the designer drugs hydergine, piracetam, DHEA, Dilantin, or xanthinol nicotinate, although decaf cappuccino still looks promising.

79. All right then; what about aroma mood manipulation?

Well, at the Shimizu construction company in Tokyo, they waft the smell of lemons over banks of keypunch editors in an effort to increase their productivity. Unfortunately, many workers can't wait to get home at night to roll on a fish.

• Deep Background:

What Really Happened to the Dinosaurs?

Dinosaurs, the most successful reptiles the world has known, flourished for two hundred million years, ruling Earth one hundred times longer than man's brief sojourn. There are several possible explanations why the orders *Saurischia* and *Ornithischia* disappeared some seventy million years ago. One scenario has Earth bombarded by the intense and fatal radiation of an exploding supernova. Another depicts a reversal in Earth's magnetic field allowing ultraviolet radiation in lethal doses to penetrate a depleted ozone layer. The theory most recently in vogue is based on satellite evidence of a huge impact crater in the West Indies, suggesting a meteor strike of such magnitude that huge clouds of dust were sent skyward, causing a "nuclear winter" and sealing the dinosaurs' fate.

The most poetic possibility posits that the evolution of flowering plants from the more primitive gymnosperms deprived the dinosaurs of certain essential oils found only in the naked seed plants, causing the dinosaurs to perish due to a rather monumental case of constipation. This would account not only for the extinction of the orders, but for the surprisingly small size of fossilized dinosaur dung.

---

80. Is the universe older and larger than thought, smaller and younger, or about what you'd expect?

> *Younger and smaller. You guessed it: It's the Hubble Constant again, the value of which is anything but (see upcoming "Deep Background: How Old Is the Universe?"). Now they're telling us it's only eight billion years old (not twenty) and only half the size. Next they'll be telling us it's an immaculate eight-year-old ranch in Hoffman Estates.*

81. Using the latest ultrasound techniques in Copenhagen, Dr. Lasse Hessel has determined which is the best (for all parties involved) position for human sexual intercourse?

> *Sideways and rear run neck and neck. And if you can do that, you can please anyone.*

82. If you would like your own nuclear blast, what will it cost you?

The bomb is absolutely free, when you pay the Chetek Corporation of Moscow three hundred dollars to twelve hundred dollars per kilogram (2.2 pounds) to dispose of hazardous waste in an underground nuclear explosion. I don't think they'll let you just go in with a kilogram, though; there's probably a minimum. This is just the ticket for people with a pile of soaked newspaper bundles the garbage man either won't or cannot pick up. (Could be he never picks up the paper.)

83. Do abalones favor brick and mortar construction for their shells or geodesic framing with a nice mother-of-pearl skin?

The former. Most abalones are extremely traditional in their building methods, which are based on stacking layers of six-sided calcium carbonate bricks using a mortar they secrete right on the site (saving a good deal of setup time). This is the reason why so many otters (who try to get these things open) die of heart attacks.

84. Is a guinea pig a rodent?

A big no! according to Dr. Wen-Hsiung Li of the University of Texas, who says that, genetically speaking, they deserve their own order of cute little things a hundred times better than rats. I really liked our guinea pig, Tony, and never understood why he killed himself.

85. What was the most amazing thing about the "Grasper," a Precambrian insectlike creature discovered in Greenland?

That scientists in 1991 found the second half of the fourteen-millimeter specimen they discovered two years before, Greenland being a pretty big place. The Grasper, which looks rather like a 540-million-year-old earwig, could be the missing link between worms and insects, if such a connection were ever needed.

86. Tell me Clemson University is not feeding cow manure to cows.

They are, but they can explain. They mix some dry shelled corn from the student cafeteria in with it, first. This is really one-upmanship on Illinois State (Normal), where they're feeding newspapers to cattle. (The bulls eat the sports section first.)

87. Did Neanderthals and Cro-Magnons date?

It's possible, but it probably ended badly, like the Montagues and the Capulets. It now seems that the two groups coexisted, although the Cro-Magnons held most of the elective offices, finally gerrymandering out the Neanderthals about thirty-five thousand years ago.

88. How hot is the hottest star?

a. *360,000 degrees Fahrenheit*
b. *510,000 degrees Fahrenheit*
c. *a million in the shade*

a. *No humidity, however, on Melnick 42 in the large Magellanic Cloud, thirty-three times hotter than the sun and so bright, the Hubble Space Telescope could see it despite its astigmatism. Melnick is spewing enormous amounts of energy and, frankly, exhausting himself.*

89.   Are octopuses dumb, or what?

Octopi. They really have a lot going for them. Unless they're just a bunch of suckers, the marine biologists at the Naples (Florida) Zoological station believe an octopus to be the equivalent of four toddlers, and can pull the glasses off the face of an entire room of adults in less than ten seconds. Possibly because they are orphans at an early age, octopi are extremely adaptable, inventive, and very talented mimes that can do a "glass wall" you wouldn't believe.

90.   Could you go back in time and interrupt your parents before they conceived you?

Well, Edweard Farhi of MIT says it's crazy, but Richard Gott of Princeton likes to flirt with the notion of blasting off on a rocket down one of two straight infinitely long cosmic strings running alongside his parents while they were mating, whipping down one string and back up the other before the tubes on the old Atwater Kent warmed up. But, that's just him.

91.   If you're recoving from a heart attack, it helps to be what?

   a. *lean*
   b. *green*
   c. *mean*

c. *Dr. Richard Milani says that people with symptoms of hostility tend to do better in cardiac rehab, although he notes that meanness may have contributed to heart problems in the first place. A little mean is good.*

92. "Just like wood" is how one chemist describes it. What is it?

> a. *oak-grained contact paper*
> b. *a green plant that makes plastic*
> c. *Plastic Wood crack filler*

> b. *It is now possible to grow your own plastic flowers!*

• Deep Background:

Do Animals Lie?

Man may be the only animal that blushes, but he is not the only one that needs to. Many species exhibit behaviors intended not merely to deceive predators but their comrades as well. Nor is the spoken lie the exclusive domain of humans: among birds, the sentinel species of the white-winged shrike tanager will cry out a "hawk" alert when it is in fact zeroing in upon a particularly attractive katydid it doesn't wish to share. The other birds are not stupid, sensing, instinctively, that a tanager rushing headlong toward a hawk doesn't add up, but, since it only takes one hawk to make a tanager a believer, the ruse is usually effective.

One has only to look closely at the mating balls in the snake pits of Manitoba to realize that something is amiss: namely, the male garter snakes impersonating females to confuse adversaries and gain a competitive advantage. Chimpanzees, taught sign language, soon use it as much to cover their tracks as to communicate: Washo, perhaps the most famous of the signing chimps, once put the blame for a lamp he had broken on a researcher who happened to walk into the room. Even insects are not straightforward: some female fireflies are in the habit of flashing mating signals to males when it isn't love they're craving, it's protein.

---

93. The "Deborah" (D) number refers to how quickly a substance:

    a. *becomes rigid*
    b. *relaxes*
    c. *stops talking to you*

    b. *A measure of viscosity named after Deborah in the Bible, who caused a scandal by relaxing on nights other than Passover.*

94. This versatile "miracle drug" can be used as a stimulant, a relaxant, or a memory and performance enhancer. Is it

    a. *nicotine*
    b. *caffeine*
    c. *Dentyne*

a. *Caffeine's good, too, but it's hard to beat the versatility of nicotine which, in small doses, stimulates, and in larger doses relieves tension (along what used to be known as the T zone, and is now known as the C zone).*

95. Is the universe a sandy beach or a bowl of oatmeal?

A bowl of oatmeal. That's why everything tends toward the lumpy, including clusters of matter, upsetting to cosmologists who believe there would be a more equitable distribution if they were distributing it. It's bad enough they can't find 90 percent of it.

96. During growth spurts, babies can grow up to

a. *one quarter of an inch*
b. *one half of an inch*
c. *three quarters of an inch*

overnight.

c. *This can be picked up on your baby intercom, and sounds sort of like the noise the inflatable pool makes when the kinks pop out as you're blowing it up.*

97. In what are one of the most important finds ever, neurologists at MIT has discovered a gene who controls which?

Grammar.

98. If you invited one of every type of animal in the world to a party, would you have to lay in more snacks for lower forms, such as worms and microbes, or hors d'oeuvres for the mollusk, shellfish, octopus, and squid clan?

You would be hard-pressed to make your mollusk friends, all eighty thousand varieties of them, happy as clams. I would just provide a little bedding for the sixty-six thousand lower forms and let them amuse themselves. Also expect: 4,000 mammals (no spouses, now!); 9,000 birds; 6,000 reptiles; 3,000 amphibians (which may be seated next to the reptiles or the mammals, according to Letitia; 20,000 fish; 4,000 starfish and urchins (which invaginate their stomachs to eat and probably should be put at their own table); 923,000 insects and spiders (a problem group: they always bring an entourage); and 9,000 jellyfishes, sea anemones, and corals so decorative one simply must arrange them around the head table.

99. Is a possum "playing dead" faking it or not?

Not, as anyone who has ever suffered a catatonic state brought on by your brother jumping out from under the basement stairs can testify.

100. Long on the back burner, the Chinese have derived a male contraceptive from what?

    a. *"Seven Happiness" seafood (#23—$8.95)*
    b. *ginseng root shaped like this*
    c. *cottonseed oil*

    c. *But when that cottonseed gets rotten, you can't plant very much cotton.*

101. Put today's modern horse and the fossil horse *propalaeotherium* together in a barn, and which would get under the other's hooves?

> *Little* propalaeotherium, *having been about the size of a barn cat. A stampede of them would have been darned cute.*

102. In a creative mood, you decide to make a planet. Assuming you can find the necessary gas and dust, how many years should you leave it in the Presto?

> a. *a few hundred thousand*
> b. *a million, or until a toothpick comes out of the center almost clean*
> c. *billions and billions*

> a. *For years, people have been overcooking their planets. The conclusions of researchers at the University of Massachusetts-Amherst are inspired by dustballs surrounding the T-Tauri stars, proving dustballs do have a place in the order of things.*

103. According to scientists in Rotterdam, what do sperm use to guide them on their way?

> a. *electrical polarities, looking for attractive opposites*
> b. *their highly refined sense of smell*
> c. *sheer pluck and tenacity*

> b. *Ever since Van Leeuwenhoek, the Dutch have been leaders in sperm science—and the hits just keep coming!*

104. Does outdoor clock accuracy correlate strongly with the speed of postal clerks around the world?

> *Yes: r = .71, a high correlation (with r = 1.00 being complete correlation) although, in a perfect world, Italian postal clerks (the slowest) would correlate to Indonesian outdoor clocks (the least accurate).*

105. Studies at the University of Chicago confirm that eating which of the following lowers blood pressure considerably?

> a. *prime rib*
> b. *lobster tail*
> c. *celery*

> c. *This shows the danger of giving National Science Foundation grants to vegetarians.*

106. Are naked mole rats competitive?

> Au contraire. *The naked mole rats of the Horn of Africa each specialize in an aspect of tunnel management as they dig for tubers; some gnaw dirt, others cart it out, and one inevitably leans on its tail and makes squeaking noises at the rest.*

107. Which is longer not to see someone—in ages or eons?

> *Well, an age can certainly seem like an eon, but an eon is longer. They go like this: Eon (Earnest); Era (Evangelists); Period (Preach); Epoch (Even); Age (to Apes).*

*An eon is about a billion years; an age, by comparison,
is no more than a long weekend.*

108. Wrapped around its esophagus like doughnuts impaled
on a sword is an earthworm's

a. *heart*
b. *mind*
c. *never you mind.*

a. *Five—count 'em—five. As hermaphrodites, they need
the blood pressure.*

• Deep Background:
────────────────

H o w   O l d   I s   t h e   U n i v e r s e ?

Astronomers recently observed a quasar that existed
when the universe was 7 percent of its current age and only
a sixth of its present size. To put this in context, it would be
like seeing me when I was three and weighed thirty pounds.
This would seem to indicate that the universe and everyone
in it are older and heavier than you had reason to believe.
Perched just a stone's throw from the edge of the universe,
the quasar, P.C. 1158 + 4635, is the most distant object ever
observed, and is thought to have been part of the galaxy-

forming process about a billion or so years after the Big Bang.

Or so is the key phrase here. As you know if you've ever tried, it's not easy independently verifying distances in the universe. You almost have to get out there with a tape measure—in this case, measuring the red shift, the increase in wavelength in the red end of the spectrum of light as stars and galaxies recede. What you want to look at here is the ratio of the velocity at which a galaxy is receding from Earth to its distance from Earth, or the Hubble Constant, so called because astronomers constantly argue over its value. Some argue the constant is ninety, making the universe twelve billion years old, and others hold with fifty, making it just a tad over twenty billion. Either way, it looks like the great cosmologist Pat Boone was right when he sang, "the years 'twixt twelve and twenty are the years of confusion and pain."

---

109.   What does a cryptozoologist look for?

Credentials. These are guys who search for Nessies and Yettis and Yentas—mythological creatures.

110.   True or false? Potatoes produce natural valium.

True, otherwise you'd never get them into the deep fryer.

111.   What do researchers at Pennsylvania State University conclude has the greatest influence on the television-watching habits of children?

a. *the size of the screen/if there's surround sound*
b. *toilet training*
c. *genetics*

c. *The controversial finding suggests that children are born with a predisposition to stare at senseless drivel.*

112. If you're the kind of person who's extremely concerned with punctuality, would you be better off buying a cesium atom oscillator or a hydrogen atom oscillator?

I think you'd be happier with the hydrogen, which is accurate to one millionth of a second per day, as opposed to the cesium, which needs resetting every hundred thousandth or so. Of course, expect to spend a few dollars more.

113. Does an oyster usually rest on its right valve or its left?

Left. If an oyster is resting on its right valve, it's feeling under the water.

114. Do adolescent ostriches feel peer pressure?

Acutely; single males hang out in gangs with whom they wander off for weeks at a time on (what they say are) communal sand-bathing binges, while the females gather in large clutches, eyes to the horizon. (You don't want to be caught with your head in the sand when the boys show up, or it's The Wild One, *ostrich style.)*

115. Does baby talk by parents slow a baby's recognition and use of language?

No, but it can the parents'. They say to speak to a child at its level of development, as long as you're not in over your head.

116. Does the spiny anteater dream?

No. Not only does it not experience the REM (rapid eye movement) state, but dreaming about ants tends to keep a guy up.

117. If you were the human body, where would you store bile?

In a tractor-trailer down the street. But I am not the human body; it keeps it right under its vest in the gall-bladder.

118. You know what they say: an old oak can produce truffles until what age?

Sixty—so odds are there's a truffle or two left in you yet.

119. How much saliva has a sheep drooled by the end of the day?

    a. *five liters*
    b. *ten liters*
    c. *fifteen liters*

c. *A truly remarkable tribute to the digestive powers of a ruminant. In fact, instead of wool, they should gather their drool.*

120. Five hundred and fifty million years ago, Austin, Texas, and which of the following were twin cities?

   a. *Santiago, Chile*
   b. *Melbourne, Australia*
   c. *Kenosha, USA*

a. *Back in the days of Pangaea—the Mega-Continent—Salt Lake City was a suburb of Melbourne; Nome and Sydney were unlikely bedfellows; and the Ross Ice Shelf was just down the road a piece from El Paso.*

121. Did snakes evolve from lizards, or did lizards evolve from snakes?

Snakes from lizards, who thought shedding their legs would be an aid to burrowing. Snakes, apparently, have never thought much of walking.

122. Speaking of snakes, if you don't wish to be spat upon by a spitting cobra sit

   a. *in the orchestra pit*
   b. *farther back on the main floor*
   c. *in the balcony*

b. or c. *They can hit you at seven feet, so you're better off with the cheap seats.*

123. During the act of procreation, does the male grasshopper become more or less amorous after the female devours his head?

> *More, silly, since the nerves just below the throat control sexual inhibition. Feminist biologists have shown great interest in the grasshopper.*

124. According to the Grand Unified Theory (GUTS), there are how many dimensions?

   a. *four*
   b. *ten*
   c. *twenty-seven*

> b. *This way, that way, like this, and seven others. Buying pants under this theory would be even more impossible.*

125. True or false? Brushing your teeth with aged cheddar cheese in a program of dental hygiene and regular professional care can prevent tooth decay.

> *True. Things must have been pretty slow in the labs at the University of Alberta to come up with this one, but it seems the cheddar "remineralizes" the tooth surface. Swiss works, too, despite having cavities.*

126. Is a banana a boy or a girl?

> *It's a girl, proving that anatomy is not destiny.*

Odds and Ends

● **SOME PEOPLE WOULD HAVE** you believe that any reference to the world's largest halibut or the mating habits of the Brady Bunch (which, in some cases, involved a large halibut) smacks of trivia. Perhaps, but Mr. Late Great Books Himself, Sydney Harris, for years made a living on newspaper columns filled with just such items (all right, not the Bradys, but the halibut; yes, that would work!) stumbled across while looking skyward for higher meanings. If knowledge were a steep rock face, these are the little pebbles dislodged by the goat-footed seekers of wisdom which come pinging down on the hood of your Festiva. They are, after all, made of the same material.

"Odds and ends"—the phrase—originally came from

all the bits and pieces (or maybe it's the other way around) a tailor has left over after trying to fit Greenberg, whose one leg is even shorter than the other (Greenberg, naturally, thinks of one leg as being longer than the other). Sometimes you have a perfectly beautiful yard or two of nice gabardine in the form of a trapezoid, which you hate to throw out, and maybe another three or four hundred like it (wools, blends, worsteds, some very nice linen, a lovely piece of imported silk only six inches short of a shirt) on the shelves until there's no room for anything else.

Let's see what you can make of them.

───────────────────────

1. If you ask for an "Arkansas fire extinguisher," what will you get?

    a. *a drink similar to a boilermaker*
    b. *a foam-type extinguisher made in Little Rock*
    c. *a chamber pot*

    c. *In Arkansas, they'll just give you a dirty look, after what they endured in the last election. Just consider it of historical interest.*

2. One of the Mario Brothers is Luigi. Who's the other?

    Mario. They could just as easily be the Luigi Brothers.

3. Did Alfred Hitchcock have a belly button?

    No, according to Karen Black, who confided to Joan Rivers that Hitchcock showed her his stomach (not just its shadow!). The master's belly button was apparently lost in surgery.

4. The initiation rite in this secret society includes lying in a coffin arms crossed over your chest and describing your sexual history. What's this cool club?

Skull and Bones, the Yale He-Man Woman-Haters' Club (and with more than one Spanky), whose illustrious members include William F. Buckley and George Bush.

5. Prince Charles is an avid collector of

a. *toilet seats*
b. *women's corsets*
c. *corrective dental devices*

a. *This is according to his wife, so bear that in mind, but Diana says his toilet-seat collection numbers well over a hundred, one of the first signs of trouble in a marriage.*

6. Where might you find the glandular secretions of the beaver besides the beaver?

a. *chewing gum*
b. *toothpaste*
c. *Liquid Paper*

a. *You could see how the brown, unctuous secretions of the groin glands of the beaver* (Castoreum) *could double your pleasure and double your fun.*

7. Saint Martin de Porres is the patron saint of

a. *cabdrivers*
b. *foundlings*
c. *hairdressers*

c. *Martyred when his mousse caught fire.*

8. In *A Midsummer Night's Dream,* Oberon squeezes the juice of what into Titania's eyes as a love potion?

    a. *toad*
    b. *pansy*
    c. *liverwort*

    b. *Even today, many New Age enthusiasts and people who attend Renaissance fairs swear by it.*

9. If a woman wants a smaller shoe size, would she be better off moving to Britain?

    Yes. A size six here is a four and a half there. Avoid the Continent, though, where you mushroom to a thirty-seven.

10. The butt, the strap, the backflap, and the cross garnet are all types of what?

    Hinges. What you don't want to do is put your butt where your backflap ought to be.

11. True or false? The largest halibut ever caught was eight feet long.

    False. The largest halibut on record was 15 feet 3 inches, weighed 726 pounds, and could be referred to as Hippoglossus *hippoglossus hippoglossus without being redundant.*

12. A ledger of George Washington's found in a Washington and Lee University vault reveals what about his financial straits?

> a. *he kept two sets of books—one for himself and one for his country*
> b. *he married money—Martha inherited nearly six million dollars (equivalent) from her first husband*
> c. *he had been badly burned in British tea*

> b. *All this and he slept in a lot of places, too (and must have run into Franklin a lot, on the way out).*

13. According to the *Whole Baseball Catalogue*, what is *nahgroodnick* the Russian word for?

> a. *a chest protector*
> b. *the pitching rubber*
> c. *spikes*

> a. *Not to be confused with nogoodnick, or umpire.*

14. The Japanese have perfected the "Flush Simulator," a recording of the sound of (one) toilet flushing. What is the rationale behind it?

> *"To conserve water by eliminating the need for cover-up flushing," and damage to vocal cords, I might add, from overloud throat clearing.*

15. Is a cat with its tail straight up happy to see you?

> *You bet. A low tail denotes relaxation or indifference; a twitching tail, excitement or irritation; and a slow-switching*

tail, a pounce in the making. No movement suggests rigor mortis.

16. True or false? Feet are referred to as "dogs" because the family pet used to do double-duty as shoe leather.

> *True. In utilitarian Colonial times the "cordwainers" were the first Hush Puppies.*

17. True or false? To find young men who had not registered for the draft, the selective service bought a list of names of children who had sent in coupons for free birthday sundaes from an ice cream company.

> *True. I suppose they have all the entries for the Flash Gordon spaceship contest as well.*

18. How long can a flamingo stand on one leg?

> *Four hours. Or maybe the reference lady might have said "for hours"?*

19. Who sells more: the round-toothpick people or the flat-toothpick people?

> *The round, four to one. Only thing is (a pet peeve), the round aren't really round anymore. They're kind of square, and make an unpleasant noise when you roll them back and forth over your teeth.*

20. When "Jimmy cracked corn," what was Jimmy doing?

Snoring. And I don't care.

21. Your mojo—working or not—is what?

A small bag you should keep with you at all times, with kind of an emergency kit of insect/animal parts and souvenirs of the person to be hoodoo'd. They've got to love you just for saving their fingernails.

22. While the cows are bellering, what are the calves doing?

Bawling. The bulls, meanwhile, are nowhere to be seen.

• Deep Background:

Who First Brewed Beer?

Although the primitive man who discovered beer was in no condition to pass on his name to posterity, he did leave a formula for banging barley seed with a stone and fermenting it in a mixture of honey and water. This primitive suds was mead, endorsed by the gods themselves, much as modern beer is by sports figures. By 2000 B.C., beer was all the rage in Egypt, where wholesalers could do a good business just supplying tombs for the afterlife where, rumor had it, a guy could work up a pretty good thirst. Egyptian beer, made of fermented barley dough in date water, was bad enough to double as medicine.

Also good for what aled you was the English drink of choice in the Middle Ages, ale, a powerful dark brew of malt, yeast, and water. While child labor and public health were completely unregulated, the strength of ale brewed and sold was strictly controlled by the ale connor. This government inspector, who wore leather breeches, would pour a little ale on a bench and sit on it. If, when he rose, the bench did not rise with him, the ale was considered under strength. This tradition survives today with the familiar sight of tavern patrons glued to their barstools.

---

23. If the national debt were a tunnel worth a dollar a mile, how long would it take for the light at the end of it to reach your taxpaying eye?

Six months, and that's with your money traveling at the speed of light. But where are you going to get a tunnel for a dollar a mile? (Light travels about 6 trillion miles in a year; the national debt, at this writing, is 3 trillion 143 billion 754 million 114 thousand 842 dollars and 11 cents.)

24. Which is the most common street name in the United States?

a. *Main*
b. *Second*
c. *First*

b. *First is sixth, and Sixth is now known as Schwartzkopf Boulevard. Park was second, and, you'll be happy to know, Third was third. Elm, due to the blight, did not even make the top ten.*

25. What is the life span of a baseball in a Major League game?

    a. *five pitches*
    b. *ten pitches*
    c. *twenty pitches*

    a. *Although it really depends on the grade of sandpaper concealed in the pitcher's mitt.*

26. Darryl Hannah doesn't eat anything with

    a. *eyes*
    b. *feet*
    c. *denim jackets.*

    a. *Or so she says.*

27. According to the *Dictionary of UCLA Slang*, what is a "team Xerox?"

    Cooperative cheating on an exam: "We did a team Xerox on the math exam because none of us had studied." This way everyone's exam gets team shredded.

28. How many times is Shakespeare cited in the *Oxford English Dictionary?*

You're not going to get this so I might as well tell you: 33,150. No wonder he thought so highly of himself. "Acid freak," by the way, appears in the OED (2), so be sure to use it in your everyday conversation.

29. When using geckos for biological control of cockroaches, figure about

    a. *two*
    b. *four*
    c. *six*

for an average-size apartment.

a. Unfortunately, you need a monitor lizard to get rid of the geckos. I don't know how you get rid of monitor lizards.

30. Fidel Castro, it was only recently revealed, has

    a. *5 houses, 32 children and 900 body guards*
    b. *32 houses, 5 children and 9,700 body guards*
    c. *900 houses, 5 children and 32 bodyguards*

b. But, in a socialist state, everybody does.

31. Every acre of American crops harvested contains how many pounds of insects?

    a. *one hundred*
    b. *two hundred*
    c. *three hundred*

a. But they're such a good source of protein, farmers should haul the bugs to market. The FDA rule of thumb is insect parts, yes; fully assembled bugs, no.

32. The head of an enemy (in season) sometimes served as the ball, and the losers lost everything including their lives in this crowd-pleasing sport. Was it

   a. *Mongolian polo*
   b. *Mayan basketball*
   c. *English soccer*

   b. *The tendency, I would think, would be to grab it by the hair and travel with the ball.*

33. *Dentate, undulate,* and *crenate* are three types of what?

   Ates. All right, leaves. And let's not forget the pinnate, serrate, and palmate.

34. What do The Bible, *Practice for the Armed Forces Test,* and *The Joy of Sex* have in common?

   They are among the books most frequently stolen from libraries. The others, according to John Maxwell Hamilton in The New York Times: Curses, Hexes and Spells; Federal Tax Reporter; The Encyclopedia Britannica, R-T; Red Pony; Birds of America *(which is four and a half feet thick);* The China Lobby in American Politics *(stolen by Chinese Nationalists in good standing); and, of course,* Steal This Book.

35. What is the latest rage in Hollywood plastic surgery?

   Breast implants for men, a "pec job," about sixty-five hundred dollars. These, unfortunately, can travel and result in Popeye arms.

36. According to Lever Brothers, how many body parts are you supposed to have?

Two thousand—and for all your two thousand body parts—finally, a deodorant soap. I only come up with thirty-six or seven, but then, I can't shower that long before the hot water runs out.

37. To conservation officers, what is a "ditch pig"?

Hunters who lie in roadside ditches waiting for geese or ducks to fly over—considered a bad practice, particularly if they do road work at night in your locality.

38. Not only did she spread the word about the toilet collection, Princess Diana let it be known she refers to her husband as

    a. *Jughead*
    b. *Fish Face*
    c. *Dumbo*

b. That's nothing: Prince Philip calls the queen Bangers, and she calls him Mash.

39. According to the Constitution, Congress has to meet once a year on January 3. What time do they have to be there?

Noon. One's OK: the roll call won't really come until two-thirty, and then there's a reception with a nice table from the beef boys.

40. Is a "fliffis" performed on a griddle or a trampoline?

Trampoline, although you might well do a twisting double somersault on a griddle.

41. What does "Vic Damone" mean to George Bush?

The hue and cry of victory at tennis, shouted in one final valiant rush at the net. Needless to say, "Vic Damone!" was not heard on November 3, 1992.

42. Which president, when offered an honorary degree by Oxford, said, "I have not the advantage of a classical education and no man should, in my judgment, accept a degree he cannot read."

Millard Fillmore. In his defense, it was in Latin.

• Deep Background:

What Was Richard Nixon Like as a Boy?

Richard Nixon was born in a lemon field in Yorba Linda, California, in 1913. When the land went bad for lemons, his father, Frank, sold the orchard. The subsequent owners discovered the lemons weren't doing well because there was so much oil in the ground.

Little Richard walked half a mile to school, had perfect attendance in second grade, skipped third, and missed only one day in fourth. Lewis Cox, his seventh-grade teacher, advised him "to work hard all the time," which he took to heart. Richard's family went to church three times on Sunday. His first piano recital, "Rustles of Spring," was deemed "creditable" by his piano teacher. According to his mother, Richard was a serious six-year-old who "reacted the same to every situation." In high-school forensics, he successfully argued the affirmative in "Resolved, that insects are more beneficial than harmful."

Although there were no indications of future greatness cited by his teachers, his citizenship teacher said that early on, Richard Nixon demonstrated he clearly knew the difference between "it would be right" and "it would be wrong."

---

43. An Italian, seeing you, attempts to bite his elbow. Should you laughingly bite yours and pull up your stool?

I wouldn't. I don't know—was he smiling?

44. According to *Working Woman* magazine, if a woman wants to lower her image around the office, is she better off wearing a sleeveless dress or a miniskirt?

A miniskirt far and away, 76 percent to 45 percent, preferably with one of those sheer, sheer blouses and a contrasting bra, possibly worn externally.

45. Who's more violent: Gummi Bears or Bugs Bunny?

I had no idea—until my daughter, Ellie—that the Gummi Bears had their own show (which also sticks to your teeth), but they do, and it's only two violent acts short of the Bugs rate of forty-nine. When Gummi Bears get violent, they get each other wet and stick one another to patio doors and kitchen fixtures.

46. According to Geraldo Rivera, was the late Sammy Davis, Jr., a Satanist?

Yes. "We have photographs of him in worship services." This from America's most respected journalist.

47. If you want to be president, you should first be what?

a. *Presbyterian*
b. *Methodist*
c. *Episcopalian*

c. *Ten presidents were Episcopalian, although a good many more were Church of England, close enough liturgically that members of each can (and do) mate.*

48. Of the 2,040 pieces of silverware in the cafeteria of the Treasury Department, how many are missing?

a. *911*
b. *1,430*
c. *1,916*

b. *Where, I might add, they are now poking their cube steaks with coffee stirrers.*

49. Shorts, skirts, and culottes worn by postal employees should not be more than

    a. *one*
    b. *two*
    c. *three*

inches above the knee.

> c. *Although the Postal Service does allow that "If any individual stands six foot four inches tall with a thirty-four-inch waist, it is likely the hem of his/her garment will fall more than three inches above mid-knee even when unaltered."*

50. Is Harry Von Zell still alive?

> *No. Unfortunately, the popular announcer on the* Burns and Allen *show died in 1981. Don Wilson, Jack Benny's announcer, in an eerie coincidence, died less than a year later.*

51. Name one thing wrong with the Liberty Bell besides the crack.

> Pennsylvania *is misspelled (only two* n's *on the bell).*

52. Is laughter the best medicine?

> *No, but medicine can still produce the best laughter. A study at the James H. Quillen College of Medicine in John-*

son City, Tennessee, found that people who were operated on listening to Jack Benny fared no better than those operated on without. Both groups still demanded anesthetics. The group that had been listening to Benny, however, did a much funnier take on the bill.

53. True or false? Among the hot new superhero figures is a green rabbit with gills who battles evil with his deadly "flatulator."

True. T. Bucky O'Hare has been called by many the next Schwarzeneggar.

54. Which is higher in calories: raisins or raccoon?

Raisins, at 289 calories per 100-gram serving, to only 255 for raccoon, that low-cal anytime-on-the-go treat.

55. What is a cow's "standing behavior"?

When she's in the moo for love.

56. Do hyenas make good pets?

Yes—and they'll laugh at anything. Although they smell terrible, are sneaky, and can break the bones of an elephant, they make "docile and trustworthy companions."

57. At the trendy Frontera Grill in Chicago, customers line up for three hours to savor what?

 a. *corn smut*
 b. *wheat blight*
 c. *root worm à la Creole*

 a. *A subtle exotic mushroomlike flavor with a corn overcast, it's "generally served in soufflés," although you can ask for a side of smut.*

58. If football were played on the width instead of the length of the field, how far would you have to run for a touchdown?

 One hundred and sixty feet.

59. Are the *reticulum, amasum,* and *abomasum* architectural features of a medieval church or of a cow's digestive system?

 The latter. Throw in a rumen *and start chewing.*

60. James Buchanan held what distinction as president of the United States?

 a. *he painted the Blue Room blue*
 b. *he was a bachelor throughout his term*
 c. *he invented the daguerreotype opportunity*

 b. *His charming niece, Harriet Lane, was his White House hostess. This distinction, despite John Updike's heroic effort, remains the only noteworthy thing about his administration.*

61. Who's first name is really "Ernestine"?

a. *Lily Tomlin*
b. *Jane Pauley*
c. *Jane Russell*

c. *Think Howard Hughes knew that?*

62. Would you call a Navy lieutenant, junior grade, *Lieutenant* or *Junior?*

Depends how much you enjoy the service. But a lieutenant commander, you call Commander, *so there.*

63. Burned toast can be used as a home remedy for what?

a. *piles*
b. *poisoning*
c. *dyspepsia*

b. *According to the* New York Public Library Desk Reference, *one half ounce of burned toast plus one quarter ounce each of strong tea and milk of magnesia is the universal antidote for poisoning when the poison can't be identified, even with the help of a reference librarian.*

64. How many full-time florists are on the presidential staff?

a. *five*
b. *ten*
c. *fifteen*

a. *Also four calligraphers, five chefs, five curators, and seventy-four people who appear to have no function—for a total of ninety-three.*

• Deep Background:

What Was It Like in the Days of Knights?

In days of old, knights were sold. Landed gentry wishing to stay that way bought protection in the form of knights errant who "paid liege" to the lord in exchange for a nice little fiefdom on the back forty. The knights signed their lives away for a period of forty days or ten thousand miles, should Crusades be involved. The chivalric code, not to be confused with charming songs sung with a French lilt, was actually the terms of the contract between the knight and the lord. The knight was obligated, for example, to defend the lord's honor (more than the lord had ever done), take his place in prison should the need arise, ransom him when necessary, and even kick in for his children's weddings.

On the battlefield, knights showed little interest in finesse, generally just seeking out someone worth macing and holding for ransom, which was considered winning. When religion flowered and the killing of anyone other than infidels was frowned upon by the Church, the Crusades were born. Knights, tired of interminably long sieges of castles and petty strong-arming, reported never feeling more like men. By the sixteenth century the knight was obsolete, as the evolution of trade and commerce created a new and ultimately more deadly soldier of fortune, the businessman.

65. According to the National Association of Movie Concessionaires training video, every patron should have "something wet, something salty, and something ———."

    a. *sticky*
    b. *extra*
    c. *noisy*

    b. *And, "Always ask a customer whether he or she wants a large."*

66. Who would win a popularity contest: a halibut or a lobster?

    Well, according to the "Popular Fish" list of the FDA, the halibut (#22) ekes out the lobster (#23), but neither holds a candle to the shrimp (#1).

67. According to Paula Voyette, housekeeper at the Houstonian Hotel, former President Bush's slippers are "big furry things" that look like they came from where?

    a. *L. L. Bean*
    b. *Walmart*
    c. *Chief Executives R Us*

    a. *The Smithsonian has dibs on them.*

68. The Hawaii Rainbows football coach attributed two losses on the road to interior decoration. What accents didn't he care for?

Pink locker rooms, which, he swears, turn players into "sissies." The one at Iowa was done up by Heyden Fry, former psych major.

69. To keep your griddle from smoking, rub it with half a

    a. *lemon*
    b. *rutabaga*
    c. *betel nut*

    b. *Making this, if John Bear in* How to Repair Food *is to be believed, the only known use for the rutabaga.*

70. Are cockateels more partial to the *Wheel of Fortune* theme or the theme from *The Andy Griffith Show*?

According to anecdotal evidence from Bird Talk *readers, Andy Griffith, although they go nuts when contestants on* Wheel *squeal.*

71. Dame Barbara Cartland's obituary, naturally penned by Dame Barbara Cartland, runs how many pages?

    a. *18*
    b. *46*
    c. *112*

    b. *And it's not over yet. In addition to "The History of Barbara Cartland and How I Want to Be Remembered," she is currently working on her five hundred and fiftieth novel.*

72. The first flush toilet was:

a. *in the tourist area at the Hanging Gardens*
b. *the highlight of the ancient Minoan civilization on Crete (2000 B.C.)*
c. *made in Flushing, New York*

b. *Prince Charles only regrets not having been there.*

73. Aside from Chief Justice Rehnquist, how many Lutherans have served on the Supreme Court?

a. *none*
b. *five*
c. *scads*

a. *Episcopalian/Church of England far and away lead the league, thirty-one to the Presbyterians' seventeen. For the record: thirteen Protestants, nine Roman Catholics, five Jews, four Baptists, and a few who never made their intentions clear. What used to be the Jewish seat on the court they'll let anybody sit in now.*

74. The Vestal Virgins used what for the perpetual fires?

a. *oak*
b. *hemlock*
c. *gentleman callers*

a. *I'll accept "c" as well, since we never did find out what happened to the guys who wouldn't take no for an answer.*

75. True or false? The ancient Greek Pithyllos "the Picky" kept his tongue in a bag between meals to preserve its sensitivity.

> *True, according to Margaret Visser in* Much Depends on Dinner. *Then there was Aristoxenus, who used to put his salad dressing on the lettuce while it was still in the ground so that it would be crisp when he picked it.*

76. How many mice would it take to equal the milk production of one Holstein?

    a. *six thousand*
    b. *ten thousand*
    c. *one hundred thousand*

> a. *And the little stools are a bitch, too. Mice are being milked at the University of Wisconsin in the never-ending quest for designer milks.*

77. Are doctors in the United States more likely to get air fresheners and lollipops or combs and emery boards from pharmaceutical companies?

> *Combs and emery boards, although my brothers, the pair o' docs, say they still get the cool full-color dissected-people calendars that kept me from even considering a medical career. In Britain, by the way, doctors are most likely to get plastic model spines—at least something useful.*

78. According to the *Dictionary of American Regional English*, does *fly low* in New England mean to walk with your head hung low or your fly open?

> *The latter, which can result in the former.*

79. Does postal insurance cover the cost of crickets that die while being mailed?

> *Yes—if handling delays cause their untimely demise; see DMM 149.251d. Remember, when mailing crickets, to use 275-pound-test double-wall corrugated cardboard, and ventilate.*

80. Mark Twain's shirts buttoned where?

> a. *on the side*
> b. *in the back*
> c. *in the front, but backwards*

> b. *His own invention. When the buttons were missing, he used to throw them out the window and yell* Mark Twain! *(From* Mark Twain's Own Autobiography*).*

81. When's the last time a dog could climb a tree?

> a. *during the Chou Dynasty, when they had it bred out of them*
> b. *they could do it now, if they wanted to*
> c. *forty million years ago*

> c. *The little tree-climbing carnivore* Miacis, *godfather not only of dogs but bears, wolves, and raccoons.*

82. "Because their tunics kept blowing up" is the plausible explanation why medieval men

> a. *wore bucklers*
> b. *wore codpieces*
> c. *brandished swords*

> b. *And c. 1340, men in miniskirts carried swords, and women discovered decolletage. The problem with codpieces was that they laced up the same as, and were adjacent to, coin pouches, and gentlemen sometimes gave the wrong change.*

83. Jose Canseco hits a ball so hard it explodes. Are the remains legally in play or is play suspended?

> *In play. Fortunately, Canseco running gives each infielder enough time to grab a fragment and see if he's got the biggest one.*

84. What does Norman Mailer generally wear on the streets of New York?

> *A safari suit and sneakers, much as you'd expect, according to Diane Johnston of the New York Public Library, who adds (quite unnecessarily, I think), "He looks like a real sloppy guy, kind of overweight." (Linda Richardson in* The New York Times*)*

85. The ladies' basketball team at Adair-Casey High School in Adair, Iowa, is called

a. *The Lady Threshers*
b. *The Lady Hombres*
c. *The Lady Bombers*

c. *YES!*

86. How do you reach Billy Joel?

Write him, care of:
CBS Records
61 West 52 Street
New York, NY 10019

87. Do new pickle regulations allow more or less stem?

Less. The USDA has been cracking down on stem lengths in its new pickle standards. Ketchup has been slowed from nine centimeters per thirty seconds to seven centimeters per thirty seconds, because too much of it was getting away.

88. Why did the book *Great Cakes* have to be recalled by its publisher?

a. *its pans were rusty*
b. *it suggested garnishing your great cakes with lily of the valley*
c. *the Bundt cake explodes if you turn it upside down*

b. *Which is poisonous. Another reason for not eating the garnish.*

89. When asked, "What odors cause you to become nostalgic?" people born in the sixties and seventies recited which litany of smells?

> a. *hot chocolate, cut grass, soap, tweed, burning leaves, split-pea soup*
> b. *Cordite, grease, the sweat of many men, cigar smoke mingled with mud in a foxhole*
> c. *Play-Doh, chlorine, ferns, tacos, baby aspirin, suntan oil and Windex*
>
> c. *Everyone has a smell they associate with their hometown, too. For me, Milwaukee will always be the hoppy days of Red Star Yeast.*

• Deep Background:

Who Was the Feathered Hero of World War I?

The undisputed title belongs to a pigeon named Cher Ami, stationed with the American forces in the Argonne Forest in France. The so-called Lost Battalion was being pounded by German, and mistakenly, American, shells on October 4, 1918, when Cher Ami was sent aloft in a desperate attempt to rectify the situation.

Spotted by German gunners and mistaken by American

gunners, the gamecock flew into a wall of fire. Struck immediately outside the perimeter, the pigeon went down, but refused to stay down, again taking to the shrapnel-filled sky on a wing and a prayer. Again the pigeon was hit: first in the left breastbone, next the right leg, then the left wing, but Cher Ami kept flying until finally collapsing in a bloody heap on the roof of division headquarters twenty-four miles from the lines. Hanging from the ligaments of his leg was the message: "Our own artillery is dropping a barrage directly on us—for Heaven's sake, stop it!" They did, and the day was saved.

Cher Ami survived to receive the Croix de Guerre from France, and retired to Fort Monmouth, New Jersey, where he died peacefully on his perch. Today, he is the only veteran of World War I on display at the Smithsonian.

---

90. Do the people of Chicago want a young or an old Richard Daley on a stamp?

Old. The young one's got a way to go yet. (He gets the syntax wrong, but, somehow, it's not funny.)

91. Ernest Hemingway was rejected for military service due to

a. *flat feet*
b. *bad eyes*
c. *ambivalent sexual orientation*

b. He did volunteer for ambulance duty in France and Italy during World War I, and came away with a bad leg, as well. Being played by Gary Cooper (in the Spanish Civil War), however, proves the sun also rises.

92. According to Don Featherstone, the acknowledged First Cause of the lawn-flamingo craze, what is the ratio of plastic flamingos to real ones in the United States?

    a. *one to one*
    b. *seven hundred to one*
    c. *one thousand to one*

    b. *There are no data currently available on the ratio of cutout bendy-over ladies with polka-dot bloomers to real ladies with the same, but, when it comes, be prepared to drop your copy of* Harper's *in surprise.*

93. Despite the fact that it no longer exists, or perhaps because of it, Pan American Airline stock now trades for how much on the New York Stock Exchange?

    a. *$100*
    b. *$31*
    c. *$4*

    a. *Coming in on a wing and a prayer.*

94. What is a canola?

Canola, Brassica napus, *used to be known as* rape, *the oil of which was used primarily as a lubricant when bear grease was out of season. Rape oil was determined by market research to lack considerable appeal to the consumer/ housewife.*

95. Which is more valuable: baseball cards or baseball card wrappers?

> *If you're one of the smarties who said* wrappers, *you're probably saving Milk-Bone dog treat boxes as a hedge against inflation, aren't you? It makes sense, I guess, since wrappers get thrown away, but really, this is getting out of hand. It's bad enough my brother Howard will never forgive me for giving his baseball cards away, despite the fact he can afford to buy them back at list.*

96. What, according to an enthusiast, does nothing but "eat, rest, and copulate"?

> Eddie Murphy *and* Aplysia, *the sea slug. If the Bible said, "Go to the sea slug, thou sluggard," you'd be hard-pressed to live up to the hermaphroditic stirrings of the chain-copulating little fellow whose mating orgies make Woodstock look like a cartoon character.*

97. Just in case you wanted to try to keep up, anyway (see above), what advice does Diane Brill give in her book, *Boobs, Boys and High Heels: Or How to Get Dressed in Just Under Six Hours?*

> *"Giggle, wiggle and jiggle," and use chrome polish on your rubber dress.*

98. Is there such a thing as kosher steel?

> *Yes, and thank God for the* mensches *at U.S. Steel in Pittsburgh for lubricating their can steel with vegetable*

*oils. But you have to feel for the inspector in the beaver
hat and the black robes next to the smelter.*

99. What color is Huckleberry Hound?

*Bluish. But, according to a spokesman for Ted Turner's
Cartoon Network, "there's nothing ethnic about him."*

100. Do retailers put small sizes on lower shelves and large
sizes on higher shelves, or vice versa?

*Vice versa, so short people cannot reach their sizes and large
people have to bend. Contrary to popular belief, however,
those triplex mirrors are not the fun house variety. You
actually look that way.*

101. Can soot, pine tar, camphor, turpentine, tallow, and
lard be used to make a wonder drug?

Yes, according to Hoosier Home Remedies *(Varro E.
Tyler) all of the above work—at least back home in
Indiana—as a poultice to break up congestion, if not fam-
ilies, and fumigates the house to boot. A more appealing
cold remedy cited is the "two hat" cure: first, hang a hat
on the bedpost, then drink whiskey until you see two hats.*

102. What do you call a dummy used for carnival ball tosses?

*A "modoc." The confusion comes from the fact that the
term is also used for someone who joins the air force for
favorable publicity. (Mrs. Byrne's Dictionary).*

103. How many bids has Harold Stassen made for the presidency?

Ten, so far. What he has in his favor are no (living) sex scandals.

104. Milk-based paint should smell like what in the can?

a. *cottage cheese*
b. *dog paws*
c. *citrus*

c. *If it doesn't, your dining room can smell like "really bad compost and body odor all mixed up together," according to one homeowner who didn't get to it quickly enough. Fortunately, she had friends she could stay with for three months.* (Chicago Tribune)

105. Who did more UPMs—*ums* per minutes—Dan Quayle or George Bush?

George Bush: 1.7 to Quayle's .1. University of California-San Diego psychologist Nicholas Christenfeld attributes Quayle's nearly um-less speech to "not contemplating many options when he speaks."

106. Do hemlines correlate with the Dow Jones averages?

Yes—both up in '65 (miniskirt), down in '70 (calf-length), up in '73 (hot pants), down in '75 (long skirts), and steadily rising throughout the eighties. The anomaly was the crash in the fall of '87, which caught women with their skirts up and analysts with their pants down.

107. Can your hair rust?

Yes—and no, and not because you have Brillo hair. Mix hard water with certain chemicals found in hair dyes, and don't it turn your blond hair orange? A hydrochloric acid rinse, of the type used to derust toilet bowls, seems to help.

108. What weighs 200 pounds and comes from Hope, Arkansas?

The world's largest watermelon, which, at this writing, still has 15 pounds on President Clinton.

• Deep Background:

What Causes a Stock Market Plunge?

The stock market plunges under two conditions: (1), because things are getting better, or (2), because things are getting worse. This arises when the economy is either heating up or cooling down, evoking a strong dollar, which is bad for exports, or a weak dollar, which is bad for everything else. When unemployment drops, Wall Street suffers fear of inflation, but when people are out of work and not spending, impetus is lent to the recessionary spiral. This is because free-market economies dictate that when demand is high, prices go up because you can get it, and when demand is low, prices go up due to higher per-unit costs passed along to the consumer, who is (1) not spending enough, and (2) not saving enough. Flaccid leading indicators cause a lack of confidence in the private sector, impacting on a scenario wherein, say, foreign car prices go up and domestic car prices rise to prove they're as good as foreign cars.

Now, you could put more money in circulation, but the Fed is as reluctant to lower interest rates and fuel inflation as it is to raise interest rates and chill business expansion, which would send shock waves through the Dow Jones Industrials causing stock prices to plummet from one of two causes: (1) because things are getting better, or (2) because things are getting worse.

---

109. Gloria Estefan reports that the predominant brand of men's shorts thrown at her during concerts is

   a. *Fruit of the Loom*
   b. *Calvin Klein*
   c. *Towncraft (Penney's)*

   b. *Naturally, a guy, hoping to impress, would be careful about which brand of underwear he tossed. Gloria is one of the few entertainers who cares enough to read all her fan mail.*

110. Are crack-crazed squirrels attacking joggers in New York's Central Park?

   Not yet, according to The New York Times, *rebutting a claim made by the London* Times. *Squirrels on crack would exhibit the same behavior, anyway.*

111. According to the U.S. Postal Service, "Delayed delivery times result in" what?

> a. *tax-paying consumers' frustration*
> b. *a blot on traditions dating back to the Pony Express*
> c. *more consistent service*

> c. *Goes to show you, consistency isn't everything.*

112. Around here the cable company still uses a brick through the window, but the interactive Queens, New York, cable franchise has devised what to discourage the pirating of premium cable channels?

> *An electronic bullet, which, in tests, shattered a row of porcelain dolls on the Home Shopping Network.*

113. Michelle La Chance of Lincoln, Nebraska, has sold a what that resembles Mickey Mouse to the Disney people?

> a. *potato*
> b. *rhino horn*
> c. *chicken tumor*

> a. *If you have anything,* anything *that looks like Mickey, don't have it removed before you give them a call.*

114. Just in case you thought the war left Saddam Hussein unfazed, *Time* magazine notes that before Desert Storm, Saddam was blinking at the rate of twenty-five times per minute. Recently, he was seen blinking how often?

a. *forty times per minute*
b. *sixty times per minute*
c. *one hundred times per minute*

a. *Saddam reportedly has a nostril that twitches once in a while, as well, but it might just be mustache irritation.*

• Deep Background:

Why Are There Acronyms?

Acronyms stem from the nearly pathological predisposition of military and government agencies to render even the most innocuous communications unintelligible. The service branches and NASA show the most cupidity in their use, CUPID being an acronym for "Contractor Using Price Incentive Doctrine." Oftentimes it's not clear which came first, the project or the acronym. Consider STORC, the "Self-Ferrying Transoceanic Rotary Wing Crane"; or SATAN, the "Sensor for Airborne Terrain Analysis." There probably would never have been a "Space Cargo Handler and Manipulator for Orbital Operations" unless it spelled SCHMOO. Ditto for FLOP, the "Floating Optical Platform"; SNAP, the "System for Nuclear Auxiliary Power"; MOP, a "Model Operational Plan"; POP, to "Purchase Outside Production"; and the onomatopoeic PLOP, a return to the "Prior Level of

Prioritization." Nor would it surprise those in the know should NAG find MUD on RUMP, since it's merely the "Naval Advisory Group" supplying "Material Usage Data" on the "Radio-controlled Ultraviolet Measurement Program."

Still, potential SNAFUs abound should you wonder, for example, whether SS meant safety supervisor, same size, samples per second, security subsystem, separation system, ship service, signal strength, simulated strike, single shot, sliding scale, solar system, solid state, space science, space simulator, special service, spin stabilized, stainless steel, stationary satellite, steamship, stock size, storage site, straight shank, strategic support, submarine sector, subsystem, sworn statement, sunset, or a reunion in Bitberg you'd just as soon miss.

---

115. Which has a bigger readership: *Bon Appétit* or *Weight Watcher's Magazine?*

Bon Appétit, *1,355,000 to 1,007,000.*

116. Gerald Ford's boyhood home in Grand Rapids has been sold for how much?

a. *half a million dollars*
b. *one dollar*
c. *three thousand dollars*

c. *Well, it needs a lot of work.*

117. Lovers of vintage models will be crushed to learn that their car is now all the rage at Monster Truck car flattening events. Which car is it?

The lovable and sturdy little Volvo. Owners are so devoted that many times they cannot be removed from the vehicles before the Monster Truck clambers over.

118. Bull sperm is distributed in units known as

a. *fifths*
b. *straws*
c. *shots*

b. *Not your soda shop variety, but tubes immersed in stainless-steel containers of liquid hydrogen. Hey, you don't just turn on the tap to get the stuff.*

119. John Deere invented

a. *that shade of green*
b. *the steel plow*
c. *the steam table*

b. *John Deere tried to trademark that shade of green, though, but to no avail.*

120. Did the Brady Bunch date one another?

Hey, this is definitely trivia. Well, all right, yes, they did, which means reruns can be viewed with a whole new twist. Greg, who wrote the book, said that he dated Marcia as well as Mom (Florence Henderson, you'll recall), whom he described as "a totally white-hot babe." Meanwhile, Bobby and Cindy were in Tiger's doghouse half the time, and the cops found Peter and Jan in the back of an Econoline. There, that's it, no more.

121. What's a gibbous moon?

That's more like it. Gibbous is a nice way of saying a humpbacked moon, at two-thirds full. Songs have been written about every phase of the moon except the gibbous. Care to take up the challenge?

122. Eye Pus, Snot Shot, Puke Shooter, and Loaded Diapers, to name just a few—of what?

Kenner's way cool Savage Mondo Blitzers action figures, which people with similar names objected to.

123. Under an Administration that was said not to have cared, a government agency was set up with a twenty-four-hour hotline for anyone who woke up in the middle of the night with an urge to do what?

    a. *use drugs*
    b. *commit a violent act*
    c. *buy stamps*

c. At face value—plus a three-dollar service charge, for all the added convenience. For two dollars more, a man comes over to lick your stamps. It's 1-800-STAMP-24, not to be confused with 1-800-WHAK-NOW (the Whad'ya Know? *Hotline) or Jerry Brown's 1-800-WHERZ-HE?*

124. What well-known public figure characterized himself as "a cross between Albert Schweitzer and Arsenio Hall"?

You'll never get this one: Mr. Rogers, as told to Parade
*magazine. This is a subtle hint that there are depths to
Mr. Rogers we will never fathom.*

125. The end of a romantic era in railroading was signaled
when Amtrak, the caretaker of America's once-great rolling
stock, reluctantly announced an end to what?

    a. *the* Master Builder
    b. *the* Zephyr
    c. *the dumping of toilets over the trestles whenever they
see a fisherman.*

    c. *But the grass sure do grow green along the tracks.*

126. Why "Happy as a clam"?

Because the full expression, according to the Dictionary
of American Regional English, *is "Happy as a clam at
high water," when no guy with high-water pants can dig
them.*

127. The greatest writer of all time is

    a. *Stephen King*
    b. *William Shakespeare*
    c. *Mark Twain*

    a. *According to a Gallup Poll: Twain and Shakespeare
are tied, with Tom Clancy for fifth. Ask me again in five
hundred years.*

Afterword

Learning Theory and Practice

● **NOW THAT I GET** to exercise parental discretion, I'm naturally tempted to give my daughter all the benefits of Psychology 101 by raising her *au naturel* in a climate-controlled Skinner box, where her every response will have been scientifically stimulated and reinforced in a clear plexiglass Eden. On the other hand, a daughter who pecked constantly would be redundant in an environment where mommy is willing to do it without reward. Sure, I'd still like to perfect a child, but now I'm leaning toward doing it in the old-fashioned way: in three or four attempts. Besides, to create a genius, you really need a genius in place; doing the John Stuart Mill thing would mean I'd have to learn Latin and Greek myself, and you know what they say about old dogs and new glyphs.

Then, of course, there's the genes, which I dispensed without really having thought it through, or at least I would have made some of mine dominant. Her mother, of course, doesn't have a recessive gene in her body, unless it's the one for yardwork. Having watched our little chestnut fall not too far from her branch of the tree, I have to weigh in on the side of nature, and not merely because it's a lot less work than nurture. Ellie, at twenty months, needs only a few easily acquirable skills and a little polishing of the incessant poop references (which, admittedly, I encourage, being middle-aged and concerned about any process that can ruin your whole day), and she'll be as well rounded as anyone else around here. Her day-care stints have already given her a leg up on socialization, although I'm a bit disturbed at her insistence on nationalizing the steel industry, despite the British experience.

Since I never had early child development (my own included, having sprung full-grown from my father's accounting ledgers), I'm not entirely sure which stage my daughter is entering or leaving at any given time, but I know she's riding shotgun on it. Where before have I seen such single-minded, unshakable insistence on one notion to the exclusion of all others? (Oh, hi, dear, I didn't hear you come in.) So much for clean slates. Not only do you not get to write on a *tabula rasa,* before you know it, she's writing on your *tabulae rasae,* and you have to buy new ones and hide them. Maybe I've got this all backward, but it seems to me my job is to find out what she knows and learn it from her. So, I read and reread all her books (I like Spot books the best: he has a very eclectic collection of friends, including Steve the monkey and Tom the alligator, all of whom enjoy one another without the endless sarcasms of Gary Larson's anthromorphs), while learning to enjoy little pleasures like collecting fuzz from the carpet, cigarette filters in the park, and rubber bands the paper boy dropped in the alley, which we loop over our wrists in a show of pride and prowess.

Live and learn!